RIGHTSIZE
YOUR HOME

THE EMPTY NESTER'S GUIDE TO
A STRESS-FREE DOWNSIZE

BELINDA WOOLRYCH

To my dear Daniel and Kathryn, Henry
and my wonderful family. For your love, belief
and unwavering support, thank you.

"What a wonderfully practical book full of excellent tips and strategies to embrace the next stage of life. Belinda has captured the essence of what holds most people back from "Rightsizing" their home and given us the tools and motivation to overcome the obstacles with ease. Well worth reading."

Rich Harvey, CEO & Founder, Buyers' Agent, www.propertybuyer.com.au

"It's no surprise that Belinda Woolrych has finally written a book about property – if you only read one book this year, make it this one!"

Geoff Grist, Residential Sales, Richardson & Wrench

"It is refreshing to get a different approach on how to present a home. As much as it is difficult to hear that some special treasure just doesn't do it anymore, it's welcome advice and we have certainly acted on your suggestions."

Peita

"You gave us wonderful ideas on how to present the house for sale. It was no longer our home but a 'business transaction' and we took your ideas on board and worked very hard to create a beautiful house for sale."

Janice

"I have co-presented with Belinda on a number of downsizing seminars now and have clients who have also utilised Belinda's services and spoken highly of the experience and success they have achieved as a result of her skills and services. Belinda is a highly motivated, passionate and skilled professional who I would have no hesitation in recommending."

Jenny Simmonds, Certified Financial Planner

"Congratulations on combining your wealth of experience, and knowledge to provide Empty Nester Australians with a practical guide to 'Rightsizing'."

Linda Coskerie, Principal, Property Focus In Sydney

"Feedback was great, thanks again for such a great event. I loved how interactive everyone got, and the fact that they were sharing their stories was a testament to how comfortable and engaged they felt - so that's fantastic!"

Mikaela Prentice, Stockland Retirement Living

"Moving at any time is likely to be a stressful activity. Especially when the move may require downsizing & sorting through many years of memories & collectables. So Belinda's book is not only a great guide to anyone about to embark upon this move, but it's a practical 'How to' manual that steps you through the practical issues. If you're contemplating such a move soon, make it easy & read Belinda's book first."

John McGrath, CEO, McGrath Estate Agents

RIGHTSIZE YOUR HOME

There's an assumption that when your children reach adulthood, have their own lives and move out of the family home, you will instinctively 'downsize' and move into a more appropriate-sized dwelling.

You will carefully sort through and cull or distribute treasured items gathered over the years, sell your home and move into one that is more suitable to your needs and much easier to maintain.

This is not always the case and for many reasons, letting go of the family home can be put off for years or not addressed at all.

Primarily, understanding that your health and well-being may be at risk by continuing to live in a home that may not suit you is why I have decided to write this book. The idea is to help you feel more positive about your next move so that you can enjoy the next stage of your life and make the most out of your retirement.

Once you believe in yourself and understand you're doing the right thing, the process will become much easier, and you will be able to transition with ease.

Belinda Woolrych
Downsizing Expert. Keynote Speaker. Author.
Educator. Advisor.

Rightsize Your Home, The Empty Nester's Guide To A Stress-free Downsize
First published in Australia in 2014 by Belinda Woolrych
(Property Makeover Academy Pty Ltd)
Suite 16, 1 Mona Vale Road
Mona Vale NSW 2101
Visit our websites:
www.propertymakeoveracademy.com.au
www.belindawoolrych.com

© Belinda Woolrych 2014, 2018

Revised edition - Version 3 © Belinda Woolrych, April 2020

All rights reserved. No part of this publication may be reproduced, stored in a retrieval system, or transmitted in any form or by any means, electronic, mechanical, photocopying, recording or otherwise, without the prior written permission of the publisher.

National Library of Australia Cataloguing-in-Publication entry:

Author:	Woolrych, Belinda, 1973
Title:	Rightsize Your Home, The Empty Nester's Guide To A Stress-Free Downsize/ Belinda Woolrych.
Subjects:	Property, Lifestyle

Author photo by:	Angela Cushway, Willowbelle Photography, Sydney
Cover Design by:	Julia Dyer, Melbourne
Layout Design by:	Julia Dyer, Melbourne
Edited by:	Julia Dyer, Melbourne
Special Thanks to:	Julia Dyer. Joanna Benzon, Di Cartwright, November Gray Deanne Bennett, Jenny Simmons, Richard Harvey

Any general financial advice contained within this book does not consider your individual objectives, financial situation or needs ('Circumstances'). Nothing in this book is intended to be investment or personal financial advice or a recommendation to invest in a financial product. Before making any investment decision, you should consider the appropriateness of the information to your Circumstances and read any applicable Product Disclosure Statement ('PDS').

CONTENTS

CHAPTER 1

The Empty Nester's Dilemma – Is It Time To Leave The Nest?   13

Resource: My Bucket List   33

7 Secrets to Enjoying Moving From The Family Home - Part 1   37

Part 2 - Tear out section for your support team   45

CHAPTER 2

Setting The Flight Plan – How And Where To Fly   53

Resource: My Property Wishlist   56

CHAPTER 3

Rightsizing Made Easy – Getting Ready For Take-Off!   101

Resource: Online Walk-Through Appraisal: Areas of Opportunity   113

Resource: Example Blank Floor Plan of Possible New Home   117

Resource: Example Unwanted Items Disbursement List   121

Resource: Decluttering and Presentation Hours Allocation   124

CHAPTER 4

The Pre-Sale Nest Makeover – Attracting The Flocks   143

Resource: Inspection Ready Tips & Tasks -
Your Last Minute 'Get Ready' Guide!   159

Resource: Example Pre-Market Preparation Calendar   168

CHAPTER 5

Feathering The Nest – New Nesters' Success Stories   169

About Belinda Woolrych   178

Resource: Moving Checklist   183

Introduction

Feeling trapped in an Empty Nest?

Stop feeling guilty about leaving home and get Rightsized for a better life!

Welcome! Thank you for choosing to read my book. I'm really excited that you're here. I've written this book specifically for those who are still residing in their family home and considering a downsize at some point. *Is that you? Or are you helping someone who is?*

You may be single or a couple; you more than likely have children who are about to or have already left home to make their mark on the world. Your home, purchased when your children were either much younger or not born yet, no longer serves the purpose for which you bought it.

If this in any way describes you, my hope is that by reading through the pages of this book, you will not only find the help and answers you're looking for, but you will also be left feeling motivated and inspired to 'Rightsize' your home and life for the better!

Let me start by introducing myself. My name is Belinda Woolrych, I am a Property Makeover Specialist, Educator and Advisor in the Property Makeover Industry. I began writing this book, way back when I started my business in 2008. Since then, I've had the pleasure of helping hundreds of property owners navigate the downsizing minefield and make the best move of their life. It's what I call 'Rightsizing,' and it's a hot topic right now. I've named it, and I'm on a crusade to encourage and motivate future Empty Nesters, like you, into having a more fulfilled life and home to suit.

I feel compelled to help because I have found that the distress caused by even just the thought of making your next move can be debilitating. Rightsizing happens to be one of the most feared projects you will have to undertake in your lifetime, which is completely understandable. There is no doubt you have a big job ahead of you.

Rightsizing presents such a huge dilemma. You may have been avoiding it or you may have delayed it up until now because you have had no idea where to begin. You may be sick and tired of maintaining a large family home and even feel a sense of guilt or loss of control when considering changing your situation.

My role is to help people who need to Rightsize, regardless of their age. Some of our clients are very senior, and Rightsizing has come a little too late. Sadly, I've seen some miserable people in this age bracket, who have unfortunately lost loved ones and the zest for life. They are isolated and alone and can no longer manage on their own in their family home.

Leaving it too late can put enormous stress on Empty Nesters, their families, their friends, and the broader community. Time after time, I see the crushing impact home maintenance and responsibility has when it drains the energy and time of the homeowner. This becomes more serious as time moves on and can rapidly escalate to social isolation and loss of friends, interests, self-motivation and pride.

On the flip side, we have happy clients who, after a successful move, now have time for themselves and friends and can take up new interests, potentially leading to a more fulfilled lifestyle and improved well-being. Unfortunately, those who have left their move until it's too late have missed out on making their retirement much more enjoyable, creating a massive sense of loss.

It was through my experience of seeing people in these situations that compelled me to write this book. I hope to encourage you to make your next move sooner, rather than later. But even if you have left it a little late, you have plenty of support to help you go through the process successfully and feel much better in your new environment, no matter how old you are. I want to encourage you to do something and act now or any time from 50+, and have a home that supports the life of your dreams.

You will discover, as you read the case studies at the end of the book, the difference we have made in people's lives by helping them prepare their home for sale and maximise their profit. I have found the most joy in not only seeing how we have increased their financial gain but also in how we helped transform their lives for the better on a physical and an emotional level.

I have had the privilege to help many, many people like you who are thinking about beginning the next phase of their lives and are ready to Rightsize their home. After reading this book, you will discover the benefits of finding a suitable home - if you have not realised them already. The future will be yours to shape.

Your families will be relieved and happy to see the burden of the large family home lifted from your shoulders. They will see an improvement in your lifestyle and enjoy watching the freedom that it brings you. Overseas trips, rekindled friendships, and many other benefits will now all be well within reach with more time and more energy.

Coupled with the social side of getting this right, I also feel compelled to help other professionals share information regarding the process of downsizing, so that you feel well informed on every level.

I have witnessed the horrors of unfortunate downsizing experiences and have seen the detrimental effects poor financial advice can have; stripping those affected of the lifestyle and freedom they deserve after working long and hard throughout their lives.

It's little wonder that when approached for advice on the subject, I hear comments like these all the time:

"My daughter thinks I should go, but I don't want to, so I just don't bring the subject up anymore."

"My son thinks he owns me. He keeps telling me I should get out of this place but I've got nowhere to go as nice as this."

"My grandson tells me I shouldn't be mowing lawns or doing roof repairs anymore. But this is what I do, and I'm going to keep on doing it. They can take me out of here in a box for all I care, but I'm not moving."

I hear the same problems from overwhelmed Empty Nesters time and time again. Instead of having fun and enjoying this stage in their lives, they are often left feeling miserable and uncertain about their future, clinging on to a home that no longer serves their needs and lifestyle.

I believe that there is a time to release the burden of maintaining a large property in exchange for having as much fulfilment as we can every day. As an Empty Nester, your children have most likely moved out to start a life of their own. So why not seize the opportunity to Rightsize from the big family home and reconnect with your life goals again.

Throughout this book, I will share with you some of the journeys my Empty Nester clients have taken, including some of the funnier things that have happened along the way. I will also share many insights, answering common questions that may also be on your mind, and reveal my unique model developed to illustrate how achievable it is for anyone to Rightsize to a better life.

My goal is that this book will leave you feeling as though you are back in control of your life and what is most probably your biggest asset. I want you to be informed, prepared and ready to take on your Rightsizing project with confidence and ease.

From my experience, there are three key challenges consistently faced by Empty Nesters:

1. They are sick and tired of always worrying about maintaining their family home. They lack confidence and are unsure who they can trust to take care of this.

2. They are overwhelmed at the prospect of managing a 'Rightsize' or knowing where to begin, often choosing to do nothing at all.

3. They don't know how to maximise profit from their primary asset: their home. They are not sure of what the buyers are looking for in a home.

Are you currently faced with these challenges?

Are you concerned about Rightsizing from the family home?

Are you sick and tired of maintaining it but feeling guilty about leaving?

Is your property no longer serving the purpose for which you bought it?

Are you unsure how to prepare your home for sale in a way that will allow you to maximise your profit?

My book's purpose is to illustrate why you may be feeling so much uncertainty and to explain how you can manage this significant project step-by-step. It will demystify the many myths and provide you with a tried-and-tested process to get your downsizing project completed methodically and strategically.

It is now time to stop putting-off and start considering downsizing from the family home. I have guided hundreds of property owners through this process and have built a specialist reputation for assisting Empty Nesters in Rightsizing their property and achieving maximum profit in the process.

As you read on, I will discuss the framework and process required to coordinate the entire Rightsizing project. I also have included case studies which I'm sure you will find interesting as they can provide useful reference for your endeavours. My primary goal is to give you an easy-to-follow, concise and informative roadmap to show you the way, and to ensure that you not only survive, but also enjoy the Rightsizing transition from the family home to your new abode.

My book is broken into five chapters to guide you through your Rightsizing process:

Ch 1: The Empty Nester's Dilemma – *Is It Time To Leave The Nest?*

Ch 2: Setting The Flight Plan - *How And Where To Fly*

Ch 3: Rightsizing Made Easy – *Getting Ready For Take-Off*

Ch 4: The Pre-Sale Nest Makeover – *Attracting The Flocks*

Ch 5: Feathering The Nest – *New Nesters' Success Stories*

I hope you enjoy reading through the book as much as I have enjoyed writing it because I believe that every Empty Nester should be able to get assistance to make Rightsizing the family home a simple, enjoyable and stress-free process. Follow my lead, and we'll have you not only Rightsizing your property, but also collecting maximum profit at the same time.

I love my job and find great satisfaction in transforming homes as well as transforming lives in the process. It is fabulous to see people having more fulfilment in life and loving their new 'Rightsized' home.

New Rightsizers often share their sentiments with me. Common feelings are: *"Why on earth didn't I do this sooner, we've made a stress-free move, had fun doing it and are now loving our new surroundings."*

So if you are looking to downsize but have been putting it off and don't know where to begin, I invite you to read on and get Rightsized for a better life!

The Empty Nester's Dilemma – Is It Time To Leave The Nest?

Rightsizing Explained And The Empty Nester Defined

So how is 'Rightsizing' different from 'Downsizing'?
Let me explain...

Downsizing (verb). to make (something) smaller.

Rightsizing (verb). to convert (something) to an appropriate or optimum size.

There's an assumption that when children reach adulthood, they will have their own lives and move out of the family home. Their parents will instinctively 'downsize' and discard the possessions they've accumulated over the years, sell the house, and move into a smaller home that's easier to maintain. Often, it does not happen that way because some people choose to live in their homes until the very end. The questions are: *is downsizing the right decision for all? What are the options?*

Ultimately, your next move isn't about downsizing or upsizing. It's about what I like to call 'Rightsizing'. It's about minimising your stress levels and living in a property that suits your current needs. This could mean purchasing a smaller private property, living in an over-55's community, a retirement village or even building a new granny flat at your home. My book is specifically written to help navigate you through the Rightsizing process, so please read on and let me guide you.

So what is it like being in this Empty Nest and how on earth did I get to this point?

Now let's define the 'Empty Nester' or 'future Empty Nester'. The Empty Nester of today is a Baby Boomer (born between 1946-1961) or the generation before - perhaps someone who's been fairly hip in his or her time, loved the safari suit, wore bell bottoms, has/had peach paint in her kitchen, doesn't realise that the awesome retro lounge chairs and buffet in their home are highly sought after items on eBay, loved Petula Clark and possibly ABBA, and is more recently considering her last hair dye.

Seriously though, here is what the Australian Federal Government says about Baby Boomers:

Baby Boomers are often in a family home and are either 'couples without children' or a 'lone person' in a family home. With Australia experiencing a significant growth factor and projection in this age group and housing type, the process of planning has been well entrenched for the authorities. In fact, together with the federal and state governments, local councils are actively researching and planning regarding this significant impact in their strategic community and economic plans.

Where I lived in Pittwater, Sydney, the local council had a Social Plan with an enormous component of all seven discussion papers including references to this demography and its impact. The Social Plan significantly references planning in 'well-being', 'housing choices', 'social cohesion' and many other topic areas. In Pittwater and surrounding local government areas, there are a large proportion of the population who are 55 years or over. Some have lived in the area since the land and building boom from the 50's to the 70's.

While young families want to get into the Pittwater area, at the same time, Empty Nesters or potential Rightsizers are taking their time moving from these homes! Pittwater's discussion paper states, *"Pittwater can expect an ageing population of Baby Boomers to have a significant impact"*. The paper then goes on to say that the suburb regeneration is struggling with this occurrence.

Suburb life cycles rely upon the framework of Rightsizing to promote sustainability in all areas. If suburb life cycles can occur for the residents, this means locals (including Empty Nesters) don't have to move away from an area and can keep their connections. The areas attract younger families, the area keeps buzzing, schools and employment are sustainable, services will stay and the local economy gets better and better.

On the following page is a pictorial representation of where Empty Nesters sit within the suburb life-cycle.

A Typical Baby Boomer's Feelings:

"For so long in my life I've been in control and thinking about others – putting them first, providing, nurturing, making sure everyone else is okay, staying on top of the cleaning, the roster, the mowing, the painting, the gardens. We had the finances in order, the maintenance, the school routine to the millisecond, the meals on time, the groceries done, the dog groomed and the chickens fed ... now it feels like, suddenly, it's all different."

My research and the conversations held with my Empty Nester clients are usually consistent. I often hear comments like:

"I've lost control."

"Spent my life up-sizing and I don't want to capsize."

"Starting to feel isolated and disconnected"

"Running out of time and energy to get things done."

"My family worry about me."

"I wish they'd stop bossing me around"

"I don't know who to trust."

"Last place I want to look is in the Yellow Pages and be ripped off by some young 'upstart' maintenance person to fix this place up"

SUBURB LIFE-CYCLE

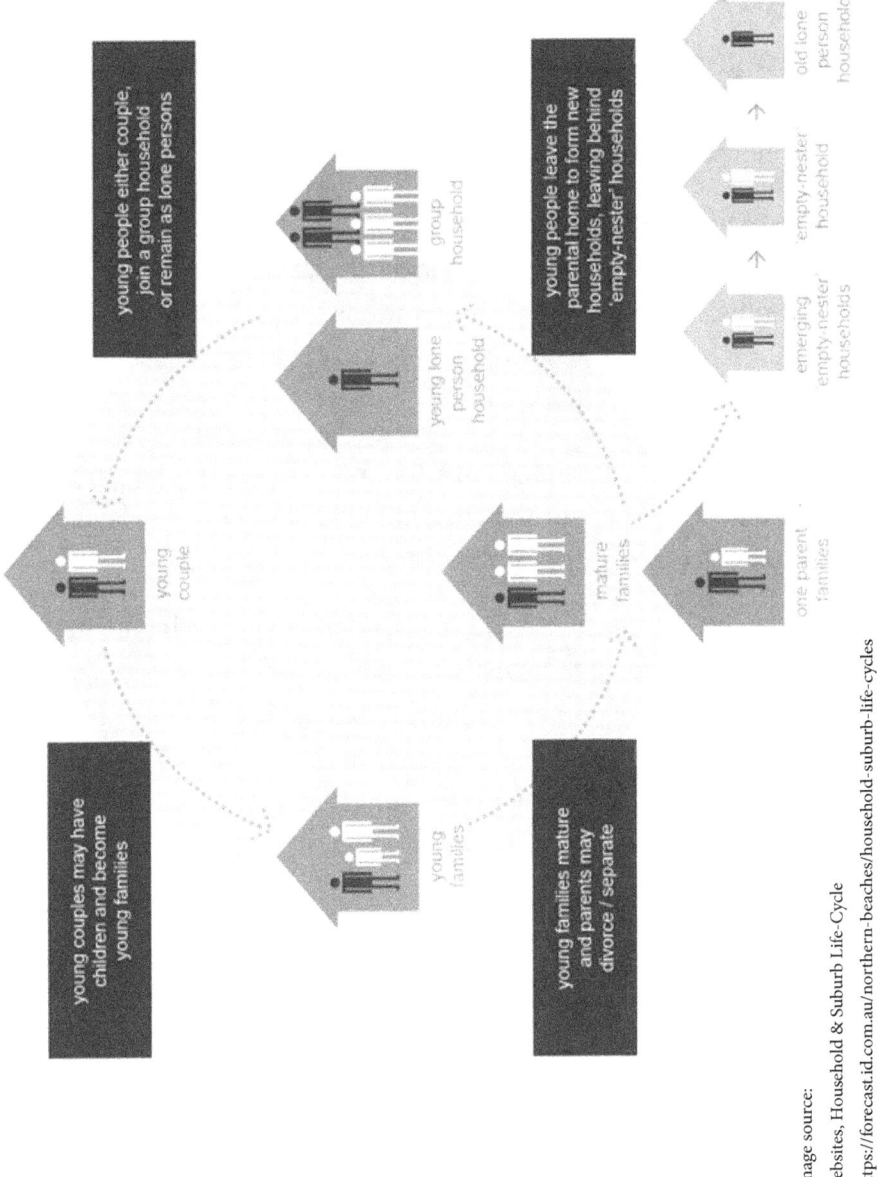

Image source:
websites, Household & Suburb Life-Cycle
https://forecast.id.com.au/northern-beaches/household-suburb-life-cycles

"Not sure what the future will hold?"

"Feeling a bit trapped in this nest."

"Starting to resent life somewhat, feeling there's no more enjoyment time."

These conversations have given me a unique insight into how people feel and I'd like to share with you the benefit of discussing a complicated subject.

As you know, the thought of giving up the family home can be somewhat daunting. *Why?* Because it holds so many heartfelt and emotional implications. Implications not only of loss, guilt, letting go and losing control, but also the subject's challenging and sensitive nature that should be open for discussion.

There is another layer of reason for the delay stemming from being a parent. Many of the current Generation Y are delaying their parent/s moving on to the next stage.

Erik Erikson was a German-American developmental psychologist and psychoanalyst known for his theory on psychological development of human beings If you follow Erik Eriksons' psychosocial stages of development, *could it be true that some parents collude with their adult children in resisting the inevitable change?*

During middle age (Erikson prescribes middle adulthood as 25-64 years and 40-64 years), the primary developmental task is one of contributing to society and helping to guide future generations. When a person contributes during this period, perhaps by raising a family or working toward the betterment of society, a sense of productivity and accomplishment results.

I feel this pattern forms due to this delayed adolescence and the parent hanging on to the children's involvement. There are perceived advantages from both sides in terms of convenience and familiarity and, of course, a delay due to a perceived belief that Empty Nesters are breaking up the family by moving on from their family home.

Unsure where to turn, and with the potential to downsize looming on the horizon, getting this 'move project' done is way too overwhelming. The Empty Nester believes that if they stay put and don't change anything from their familiar surroundings, then the problems might remain at bay.

I recently caught up with a long-time respected friend and asked her to share her insights and thoughts about this challenging subject. We have recently styled her home which she went on to sell very successfully. She is a typical Baby Boomer and has now experienced her downsize from her long-term family home, into a two bedroom unit.

Over a coffee, we discussed 'life' and how she is feeling a year into 'the other side' of her downsize. In fact, it seems she has moved through her myriad of emotions and is now enjoying the freedom of being untethered from home. With cash invested, she now has a sense of freedom that was not possible before.

One thing we discussed quite deeply was our understanding of general 'taboo type' feelings we have both seen to come from Empty Nesters. Unspoken truths begin to surface and the exploration of how one really feels about his or her situation can cause a huge amount of stress. *Do you feel the same way?*

There comes a time when you may begin to question the choices you have made or the situations you are in. An example of this may be *'do I like this job?'* or at home, *'why do I put up with this?'* or *'I wish I were spending time working on that'*.

We are also seeing a number of Empty Nesters following the lead from their delayed adolescent children way too much. We hear time and time again that children are 'coming and going' from home, and mostly being allowed to dictate the future of their parents.

Is that an excuse not to face the reality of changing a home?

Is it really the children's act of coming home and staying only twice a year the one thing that holds the family together?

Is it true that you will lose respect if you do not stay in your home as a parent, as you always were?

Are you breaking the family up by moving?

I genuinely believe the house is not the family glue. Your relationships are the bond that keeps you together.

Empty Nesters, my friend said, are often questioning their strength to take on the next phase in life. "We are 55-60+, we are very used to and comfortable with our home's surroundings, we are looking for reasons why we should stay and not why we should go." In 99% of cases, I hear that it is so much easier to justify why they should stay, rather than why they shouldn't. Empty Nesters tell me about lacking confidence for this enormous task. They don't feel as robust as they once were and are not sure if they're up to it,

Again, this resistance to change is very common and so are the misconceptions about the Rightsizing project and the true meaning of what the future holds on the Rightsizing path.

Is Now The Right Time?

When is the right time to downsize, and where do I start?

In the following pages, we will explore when and how to get started and provide you with some great tips and strategies to help you feel more positive about moving forward.

There is an enormous decision to be made in the midst of working out if it is the right time. The truth is, there is never a right time. It's the same as having children or changing jobs. You need to use your gut feeling. What I can tell you is preparing sooner rather than later is ideal. If you can plan ahead, you will experience minimal stress and you will feel more in control of the situation. Simply picking this book up and opting to read more about Rightsizing would indicate to me your journey has already begun.

I would like to pose a few questions to help you decide further if the right time to change your situation is now approaching.

Do you find it hard to keep up with maintaining your home?

Do you wish the layout was different to serve your current needs?

Does your home no longer serve the purpose you bought it for?

Do you think your place might be a bit too big?

Are there rooms in your home that remain behind closed doors?

Do you spend all weekend gardening?

Is your garden too hard to maintain?

Have you accumulated too much stuff and you worry about where it will go?

If you have answered positively to the previous questions you can probably see that it is time to make a move.

Sorting out your treasured items can be one of the biggest blockers when moving. It can be so emotional and such hard work to decipher. This is one of the main reasons people decide to stay where they are. In helping our clients declutter, we have seen everything from university paperwork to travel souvenirs, hobby and craft knick- knacks, precious keepsakes, even several pieces of fantastic artwork. Most items hold a great deal of sentimental value, and letting go is easier said than done.

I agree that it's hard to think, *'Well, how am I going to get this done?'*

I want to take it all with me but I know I can't.

Then there is that ever-present issue of, *'Who can we trust to help us through this?'*

Do you think your kids are too busy? Have they got children and lives of their own and you feel like you're imposing on them?

You are most probably thinking you don't know how you're going to fit this big project into your life or manage to find the right help.

Understanding Change

Before I became a property makeover specialist, I had a career working with one of Australia's leading retailers in the Human Resources, Training and Change Management arena. A big part of my role was overseeing a team of brilliant training designers and facilitators. The other part was extracting specific information from the minds of our senior executives, then converting that information into an adult learning framework for thousands of team members. It was a fantastic job!

I was fortunate enough to gain some incredible insights which led to some fantastic opportunities. It formed a big part of my life and helped me become who I am today.

As much as I enjoyed my role, over a decade ago I decided to change my career direction. I took a leap of faith and followed my heart and began a career in property makeovers - something I had always loved doing, on a personal level. This decision was made was around the same time I had my first baby.

It became apparent, the experience from my role as a Change Manager translated into my role as a Property Makeover Specialist, and I still draw from those experiences, every day.

Change Management is having an incredible impact on many industries in this day and age. I believe that this topic not only has a place in everyday business but also in all areas of family life. The impact of change can be detrimental if not managed in the right manner. In fact, understanding change will help you immensely in any transitioning process, especially if you are having to Rightsize your home.

At this point, it would be relevant to share a theory around Change Management you may already be familiar with. We talk about this at our Downsizing Seminars and online workshops, and it is evident that most of the audience are familiar with it. This model was based on a theory of grief cycle, by Dr. Elisabeth Kubler-Ross. She said that going through 'change' is closely aligned to experiencing a significant trauma or loss.

The trauma may be the result of a severe illness you or a loved one may be experiencing, a death within your family or a situation that has a significant impact on your life, such as job redundancy. In many cases, the process of facing a Rightsize would also cause substantial emotional stress and have a traumatic effect.

The Emotional Cycle of Change graph pictured below is based on Dr. Kubler-Ross' theory. This process represents the experience of emotions that pass when going through change.

The Kubler-Ross Change Theory

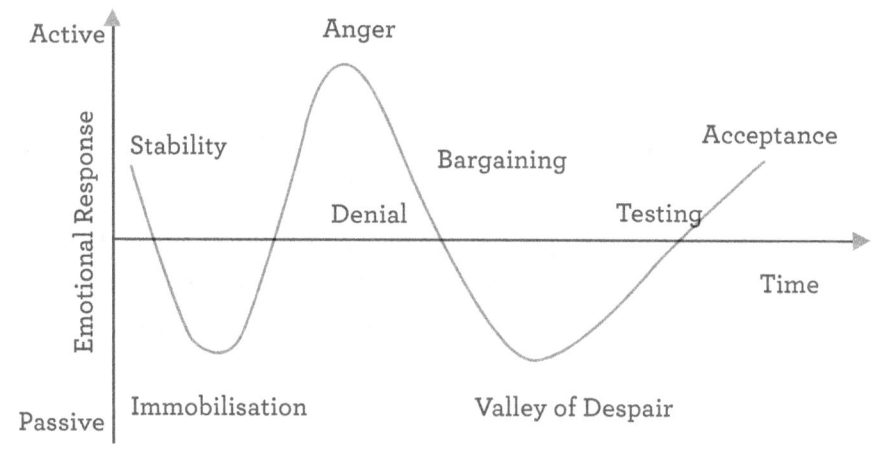

So if we liken the event of a Rightsize to major change it would be fair to say when change hits you, it's a shock. When the shock hits, our primal instincts kick in, and we become frozen. The trauma can manifest itself in different ways depending on the person and the situation. Generally, my clients tell me their thoughts are anything from feeling a loss of control to feeling guilty. As mentioned in the pages before, there is also a huge feeling of being overwhelmed.

As you can see from the graph, the spiral can continue to go down. Your family is worried and want you to move house, but you keep digging your heels in! The list goes on and next comes 'denial,' then 'anger,' 'bargaining' and sometimes even 'depression.'

I want to talk with you about the 'D' word. Yes, depression is out there. No-one is immune to feeling depressed at some stage in their life. Even if you are an incredibly positive person, a considerable change can trigger depression. Although unpleasant, is a natural part of the process and, hopefully just a phase you will move through. You may need support if you find your situation distressing. I would highly recommend letting your friends know how you feel so they can help you through it, or help you find the help you need.

I hope that by reading this book, you will think this through and tell all your friends about it, because if I can help one person understand this transition more easily, then the hundreds of hours spent penning these words would have been worth it. If I have been able to help any of your family or friends through challenging times, I will feel blessed.

I have been lucky enough to speak about this process many times for Australian Unity Retirement Living and for Lend Lease and Stockland Retirement Living. They have taken me to some of their fabulous villages around Australia (some better than the most elegant hotels I might add!), where I have met and spoken with hundreds of potential Empty Nesters or Rightsizers.

Another point to note is that moving through major change successfully is a team effort. Just like a Program Manager works with a Change Manager to implement successful programs, the same is reflected in the home where change occurs. Your friends and family may like to play their part in this change management process.

Communicating with your 'team' and gathering 'informed optimism', then formulating the Rightsizing plans (with people like us and by reading this book), takes you to the better side of the graph. Over to 'testing' and 'acceptance' as well as something that is not on there – having 'more life fulfilment' as a Rightsizer (which I'll share later in this book).

I meet a lot of my clients in the 'Valley of Despair' phase (or crisis point); however, I would like to meet you much earlier. I'd like to think that a key outcome of this book is to help you feel more positive and in control earlier in the piece, so there is less emotional stress along the way.

This requires a little planning on your behalf and the willingness to prepare earlier and in a guided and strategic manner. If you feel as though you have stumbled on this book a little too late, then please read on. I am sure you will find some comfort and advice that will help you get on top of things and finish in a favourable light, as well as understand the exciting life chapters ahead of you.

Linking the Phases and the Process of Change

Before we move on further, I would like to share another 'Change Management' strategy from Kotter, a well-known theorist in the 'change' field. The following process represents more ways of integrating change management approaches into your project to help with the process.

By this point in the book, there is a fair chance you will have guessed that I'm a real fan of creating effective change. And as you read on, you will notice some more of Kotter's strategies appearing.

The central message here is that you will need to take the appropriate steps toward your end goal, and knowing what steps will help you move forward more easily. I didn't say it was going to be easy, but it will be worth it!

As a 'Rightsizer' you should know that you have so much more enjoyment in life ahead of you! *Why wouldn't you move from the family home and discover the fun and life riches that await you?*

Potential Empty Nester Roadblocks

Your biggest stumbling block may be feeling the 'home hub' is being lost, or that you're in some way not living up to your children's expectations. In many ways, this dilemma is self-created and not exactly true.

You may feel as though you have a responsibility to your children, like keeping their bedrooms precisely the same as they were when they were growing up, or 'holding on' to their inheritance. *Does this sound like you?*

Without even realising it, you may be holding yourself back. If you are feeling pressure from your children, you will need to sit down and talk to them about your needs moving forward. You may be surprised with their response and receive their much-needed love and ongoing support.

Your children may want you to be in a smaller, more comfortable and easier-to-maintain home. They will not be fussed about keeping their rooms the same way.

Usually, the grown-up children have a place of their own or are living with their partner. They may have entirely left the nest. The best thing to do is to be aware they may have feelings towards change and need to go through their own process of acceptance.

With the children having their own busy lives, 'family hubs' can be held anywhere. You can meet at a local park or local café, at your children's homes, or at your new lifestyle or retirement village. With families often dotted all over the world, you may find yourself getting together with your family online through Skype, FaceTime, Facebook Messenger, Zoom or Hangout.

I can assure you that in 99% of the cases I have encountered, these grown-up children are saying it's not necessary to keep hold of the family property – times are 'a-changing,' and they want you to change with them so that you can have a less stressful existence. Or, if you are thinking you are 'holding on' to their inheritance by 'holding on' to the family home, it's possible that your children don't want to live in the family home.

A better option would be to 'Rightsize' your living arrangements and help your grown-up kids with the extra funds by relieving some of their current debts. You could even help them buy a home or pay off some of their current mortgages. There are many ways of 'Rightsizing' your life so your children can truly benefit.

Another common reason for not Rightsizing is that Empty Nesters are not sure where to go and don't know where (or how) to start looking.

Many of my clients are unaware that there are professionals who search for and find homes for a living. A 'Buyers' Agent' is someone that works for you. They help you find the right area, the right street and, most importantly, the right property that will suit your lifestyle and needs.

A good Buyers' Agent will help remove the stress and worry of the transition as well as negotiate on your behalf. You will hear from one of these professionals in the next chapter. He will explain what they do and how you can go about working together to achieve the best outcome.

I've seen a few stumbling blocks in my time! Some Empty Nesters are excited about the entire process and can't wait to shed the ever-consuming responsibility of owning a large property. They summon the children to come over, pick up their stuff, threatening they will toss everything if they are not there in time.

Others hate every minute of it and are reluctant to leave. They complain that their children are being pushy and resist change for the next stage of their lives.

So, have your kids left a few things behind?

Since when did you become the free storage facility for 20-40-year-olds?

If you don't need all the bedrooms and the house is literally too big and doesn't need to remain the 'family hub", isn't it time to consider making a move?

The last stumbling block is how to manage the financial side of things. We will talk about money and how you pay for the next nest, how to decide whether to sell, rent or build a Granny Flat, and lastly, we will help you with organising the big move.

***

As I am writing this, we are in the middle of strict communication protocols due to the Coronavirus pandemic. We are now living in changing times, and the 'new' way of living will soon become the norm, even when the situation eases.

The fear around contracting the virus will force people to stay in and live remotely. Our habits are changing and we will all live cautiously in the future until a vaccination is available.

The way real estate is being conducted is changing by the minute. Your home may be appraised over video or FaceTime for example. Open home inspections have been banned and online auctions are in place. The Property Market may fluctuate over the coming year, however in most cases, if you buy and sell in the same market, you will not lose out.

We are fortunate we have the technology at hand and the means to adapt to a changing landscape. Even though the process may be a little different - to get you from A to B, the end result will be the same.

Ironically, it is a fantastic time to purchase a family home. The interest rates are low, however uncertaintly will make anyone nervous about creating any sort of change.

My view on Rightsizing still remains the same. You need to put yourself first and not put off the inevitable. If you are finding your home too hard to manage or it is not serving the purpose you bought it for, you will need to address your situation.

Again, do it when it feels right for you and when you are in control of your decisions. There will be people to support you throughout the process, when the time comes.

At this point in time I know there are thousands of Rightsizers who are worried about embarking on change, however there is no time like the present. In fact, most people will be spending the time wisely, while self-isolation to declutter and prepare for their next move.

Live Life For You

By now, we should have you thinking about making the most of life and the next stage of your retirement. This section focuses on creating a vision for your lifestyle. Ask yourself, *'What do I want to be doing in my future? What is on my lifestyle bucket list?'*

If we agree that we are only really here for a short time, then as an Empty (or almost) Empty Nester, it's time to get more out of life right now. Yes, you have given yourself to others and worked hard all your life. So how about finding the inner-you and holding that as the higher-value and purpose in your life now.

Ask yourself these questions and start to focus on you and your life. You have an opportunity to map out the fun things you've always wanted to do but haven't had the opportunity to experience. It's called a bucket list. We've all heard of it. *What's on your list? Have you ever written it down?* If you want to make it happen, write yours now!

My Bucket List

Having a bucket list can be very motivational. It can help you clarify how you want to spend your time and money in the future and also help you feel more positive about Rightsizing your home.

It is a great idea to list all the fun and interesting things you want to do. When writing this list, think of the things that will give you a great sense of pleasure and achievement.

Is it going on more holidays or buying luxurious things?

My Bucket List

Things I want to do when I've Rightsized to my new place.	Due Date

Maybe it is spending more time with family and friends and doing things you love?

I heard of a lady who had been living frugally for her entire life. She was living on a big block in Sydney. When she did eventually downsize her home, she had plenty of money to spare after a successful sale when the property market was at it's peak.

When asked what she would like to buy with her excess funds, now she did not have to worry about the cost, she said that she wanted a new ironing board!

This really highlighted how much she may have missed out on by holding on to her family home. Unfortunately, she was no longer fit enough to travel.

Not so for you! Over the following pages I have provided the space to start writing your list now. Have fun and let the sky be the limit!

It's All About Me Now – Where To 'Rightsize'

Being 'all about me' means that you are holding yourself as your highest priority and, of course, your close family and friends will also be very near the top of the list. So please understand that by Rightsizing your life, you are ultimately looking after them by looking after you.

The future is so exciting when you have released the family home and the burden of owning a large property. I have clients who can now enjoy a completely different lifestyle because they have chosen to Rightsize.

One lovely couple had our team style their home and present their property for sale. They achieved a fantastic result, downsized all of their belongings and are now on the road for a minimum 12 month 'grey nomad' trip around our lucky country!

We have also worked with clients who do not necessarily want to reduce the size of their home. They want to live on one level with gardens that are easy to maintain.

One client downsized from her three-bedroom home and went to a one-bedroom retirement living apartment. Another relocated from her five-bedroom property to live near all her bridge club friends and moved into a lovely 55+ apartment. Yet another of my Rightsizers left a large apartment in a retirement village for a smaller apartment in another retirement village.

Another example of Rightsizing is the '6 months here and 6 months there' traveller scenario. The list is endless. Recently, I had the opportunity of building a stunning custom Granny Flat attached stylishly to our family home in a difficult land area. You would not have believed it was possible and how fantastic it looks. The land fulfilled the criteria to secure necessary approval through state legislation and we built it. *So why not consider building a Granny Flat on your existing property to increase your Rightsizing options?*

It can provide an excellent rental income while you remain living in the family home. When you are ready, you can possibly transition into the Granny Flat and rent out the family home or have your family move in! This way, you are not even leaving your local community if you are not ready to move into a new community.

For more information about how to manage the financial planning (amongst other things) regarding Granny Flats, see my Guest Author section (Jenny Simmonds, Chapter 2).

By preparing for your future, the 'lock up and leave' or the Rightsizing preparation means that you are securing your family's future as well as your own. It is so critical to get all your Rightsize planning started and executed while you are fit, healthy and in control of where you want to be in life. Your family will really love the idea and start to worry less about you.

Further on in the book, we will discuss the types of property you want to go to in relation to expert financial advice. We will also delve further into the pros and cons of the different kinds of places you can choose to go.

7 Secrets To Enjoying Your Move From The Family Home

Part 1 – Enjoy Moving From The Family Home
— For The Empty Nester

Part 2 – Enjoy Moving From The Family Home
— For The 'Rock' (your team)
- **Tear out and give to your support team**

7 Secrets To Enjoying A Move From The Family Home

'Rightsizing' doesn't have to be a traumatic experience for you. In this section I will share 7 secret tips for moving, settling and styling up your life.

These are my very own secrets to help you make your move as enjoyable as possible. These secrets have been designed in two parts. Part 1 is for you - the Empty Nester - and Part 2 is for those who are your 'rock' (i.e. your family and friends who are there to support you). Tear this section out and ask your support person to read and understand it. We know that effective change requires support and this is putting change management into action.

They should ensure that you take time out and look after yourself throughout the entire process so that you do not fall in a heap and can maintain your well-being. Calling on professionals to help is advisable. You want to be able to enjoy your new home and lifestyle when you arrive and not feel burnt out or exhausted.

Being informed and involved every step of the way is imperative. Aim to make this an enjoyable experience and do the best you can. This will help you minimise any feelings of regret.

Everyone has moved at least once in their life. Understand that this isn't just an ordinary move. It's a big decision to make that can affect others positively and negatively. Issues can arise, however, with the right people around to help, solutions are always close at hand.

Part 1 – Enjoy Moving From The Family Home
– For The Empty Nester

Moving may be one of the most significant events you will have in your life. It is completely understandable if emotions come into play. You will have accumulated a lot of memories and possessions in your home over the years and sorting through these is bound to stir up mixed feelings from the past. You may well have seen people come and go, lots of parties, big occasions, fun and sad times. It is important to acknowledge and savour all those memories.

Secret #1: Perception Is Reality
Acknowledgement & Facts

Acknowledge your own feelings of loss or grief for your home. Having to relocate to a new home can bring light to many feelings of life and even death. Your feelings are of the utmost importance right now. Talk things through with your person of trust. It is vital for you to express your feelings so they are acknowledged and discussed.

Know the facts about where you are going to live, even if you don't think you are ready or you haven't selected your new home, and write your lists of needs and wants about your future home. You may need to put a little thought into this if you have not visualised it before now. Be real; don't discuss the new place as if it's a brand new fairytale castle or as if it is terrible and shocking. It is about moving into a new chapter in your life. I recommend you stay positive, however, if there is sadness, feel free to let this flow. An excellent way to stay positive is to keep the focus on all of the things you want in your future home and make sure you stick to that plan. Be informed and discuss the factual details of your new Rightsize often.

Secret #2: Set The Ground Rules
Communication Must Be A Two-Way Thing

Listen to concerns. If you have not had an open discussion with yourself or your partner (if you have one) about moving, now is the time. I usually find that there is one party from a couple who is willing to come along to my Downsizing event, while the other is reluctant.

It is time to hear your loved one's concerns and for him or her to listen to yours. Communication is essential at this time and you will need to be on the same page as others to move through the Downsizing process with ease.

Secret #3: Allow Someone To Help
It's A Team Effort

Don't feel taken over unless you want someone else to look after the entire situation. It might be easy to feel pushed around, but usually your 'rock' (your team) of trust is only trying to help.

The transition may be difficult for everyone involved. Allow your team to have input and also be ready to receive their guidance. Remember that just because someone is trying to help you doesn't mean that they are trying to take over and control you. It is your home, after all. Be alert and aware of your teams' feelings towards change. They may also be emotionally attached and are also going through the process of letting go. You may not like that your family does or does not want you to move. However, you do need to look after yourself at this stage in your life. Give them this book to read. It will help them see how you are feeling and what Rightsizing will mean for you. It is essential to surround yourself with a team of genuine supporters and deal with any resistance through effective communication.

Secret #4: Sell / Rent / Build Your Granny Flat When The Time Is Right
Don't Rush Into It, Both Emotionally And For Adding Value To The Property

Don't worry about selling or renting your home immediately. These memories took time to grow and develop so allow yourself the right amount of time to move on and let go. At this stage, it is advisable to invest in some unbiased, sound financial advice. It is smart to have your property generate as much income as you can and to realise your options and the position you are in. Rightsizing effectively at the right time and having extra funds available to do this would give you a significant advantage. This is no time to rush. Working out when to sell or rent your property as part of your financial plan is imperative. My business specialises in presenting properties for a contemporary market for rent or sale. We know that dedicating time and expertise in getting the property looking right will reap the rewards if you are selling, and I would highly recommend taking every step toward making as much profit as you can. You have worked hard all of your life and you deserve it.

Secret #5: Be Positive – It's A New Chapter
Believe In Yourself

You can do this! I am sure you have been through many challenges in your life and you are still here to tell the story! You have years of experience and may have even travelled the Seven Seas. There is not much that you can't handle. Look back at all the things you have achieved. Believe in yourself and know that you CAN do this. Rightsizing is achievable for you. Your trusted team need to know that you genuinely believe in yourself, too.

Secret #6: The Cycle Of Change
Understand Where You Might Be

For an Empty Nester, making the decision (or having it made for you) to leave your home can be devastating – or it can be exciting. First, there are the thoughts of an impending move. Not everyone likes to move or leave the place they call home. The stress level in that alone can cause anxiety or even depression. As an Empty Nester who is moving to a new home, you need to be aware of the stages you may go through as you transition. It is essential to be mindful of this cycle so please have a good understanding of 'The Cycle of Change,' as we have discussed earlier in this chapter, and consider the effects.

There is also an association with moving house and moving to a new chapter of life. We are getting older and we need to understand that we are associating 'letting go' of the family home with the perceived letting go and familiarity of the 'younger you'. This may stir thoughts of *'Who am I now?', 'Am I happy moving into this chapter?', 'How will I cope on my own or with my husband or wife now', 'Are we wanting the same thing?'* and so on. You are moving out of one phase of life and are now entering a new one. It can be a daunting prospect and it can bring feelings of happiness, unhappiness or uncertainty about the future.

Secret #7: It's A Team Effort – Your Person Of Trust
Connect With Them

Connect with them. It's a team effort to work through this transition. Rightsizing is not something that happens every day as discussed in the introduction. Don't try to do it alone and communicate your thoughts and feelings with someone you want to help you through the process. The change will take time and effort and a problem shared is a problem halved, as they say. If you don't have a friend or relative who will take this project on with you, I encourage you to engage a professional team to help you through the process. Try to be involved in the personalisation of your new home.

Hiring a professional is something you can choose to do. Make sure your personal belongings are handled with the care and respect they deserve and talk through each of these items with your trusted person. Take what you want with you to your new home and ensure your other unique items are passed on to family or a new owner who will love them, too. Your new home should become more cozy with only your most treasured and loved possessions in it.

***

THIS SECTION IS TO SHARE WITH YOUR SUPPORT TEAM

Part 2 – Enjoy Moving From The Family Home

– Written for The 'Rock' (your team).

Congratulations on taking this role. Your help and guidance is critical in the downsizing process to whomever it is that you are helping. I am sure your support is much appreciated.

Those experiencing the transition and looking to find a new living arrangement or more appropriate home may not be feeling positive and can be emotionally distressed. This is all new to them and you may notice they will experience different emotions. There comes a time when the decision to move or relocate must be made for their safety and well-being. This may be a difficult time. However, it will be for the best especially if they move through the process in the right manner. You are now their confidante - the person they trust to help them make all the right decisions.

I have created the following 7 secrets to help you support your loved one or the person who is downsizing. If it all gets a little too much, remember you can always draw on local professionals to help.

Secret #1: Perception Is Reality
Acknowledgement & Facts

Acknowledge your loved one's feelings of loss or grief for their home. Often having to relocate to a new home brings to light many of their own feelings of life and death. The feelings your loved one is experiencing right now are of the utmost importance. Don't oversell the place where they are going to live. Be real; don't discuss the new place as if it's a brand new fairytale castle or as if it is terrible and shocking. It's great to be positive, however it is recommended that you are straight forward with your loved one about what's really happening. Keep them informed and discuss the details of their new home, often.

Secret #2: Set The Ground Rules
Communication Must Be A Two-Way Thing

Listen to concerns. There may be several parts of this transition you do not understand or you don't think need to happen. You need to have your ears open wide and make sure you are truly listening to all concerns. If there are some things you are not quite sure about, contact a professional and ask. You may need to engage local services to help if you cannot manage on your own.

Secret #3: Allow Someone To Help
It's A Team Effort

Don't take over the entire process unless you're asked to do so. Be sensitive to others and remember this transition is hard for everyone involved. Allowing your Empty Nester to 'drive' the project, if they are capable, is the best way you can help them transition. It is important to respect the adult. It is not a role reversal. No one is a 'child' in this scenario. It is all about adults respecting adults.

Secret #4: Sell/Rent/Build A Granny Flat When The Time Is Right
Don't Rush Into It, Both Emotionally And For Adding Value To The Property

Don't chat about selling or renting the home immediately. There are many treasured memories and possessions associated with the home. It will take time for them to move and let go of things. At this stage, it may be a good idea to mention that the memories will come with them and not be left behind in their home.

Before anything, your Empty Nester will need to invest in some sound financial advice from a professional that specialises in helping retirees. The right timing and management of the financial plan is essential. It is best to make sure you are not rushing, as it may cause a sense of concern for them. Each time they move through a new step in the process, they will feel more in control and confident.

My business, The Property Makeover Academy and belindawoolrych.com, offers a stress-free, done-for-you makeover service for the Rightsizer, ensuring their property is ready for a contemporary market. So if they are selling, they will reap the rewards and achieve maximum profit and, if they are renting it out, they could maximise their rental return.

Your Downsizer may be advised not to bother preparing their home in any way because it will be knocked down by the purchaser. However, it is worth getting a second opinion. I hear far too many stories about people buying blocks of land for a steal simply because the place being sold has been poorly presented and sold without care. Be cautious about people saying that you do not need to worry about presenting your property. Even if you are expecting your property to be knocked down by the next owner, it will likely still need to be rented out to create income for the investor while their plans are being approved.

Secret #5: Be Positive – It's A New Chapter
Believe In Yourself

You and your Empty Nester can do this! Your Empty Nester has been through many challenges in their life and they are still here to tell the story! Assure them they must believe in themselves and you know they CAN do this. It is not insurmountable.

Secret #6: The Cycle Of Change
Understand Where You Might Be

Imagine your life being turned upside down. When faced with difficult times, it can be hard to imagine the positive side of things. Your Empty Nester's perspective may be very different to your own. You may not be able to step into their shoes, but you can make sure they are well taken care of and in good hands.

As a friend or family member of an Empty Nester, you need to be aware of all the stages they may go through as they transition. It is important to be mindful of the 'cycle of change' (illustrated prior) and understand the impact you are having, as well as the situation for the Empty Nester. Ask yourself how you can best provide positive help and support toward the situation.

Secret #7: It's A Team Effort – Your Person Of Trust
Favourite Point – Connect With Them

Connect with them. Visit as much as possible and know that it matters when you are around. Ask for permission to be there and don't turn a blind eye to what's happening. Be involved every step of the way. The senior in your life needs you. Call in on them and organise family or friend gatherings often, not only on holidays and birthdays! They need your presence, not presents! Be there for them. Try to be involved in the personalisation of their new home. Make sure special belongings are being treated with the care and respect they deserve. Their new home should become as cosy and as loved as the one from which they have just come from with all of the most important items in there.

***

Some Common Concerns

Several things may worry your loved one when transitioning to a new home. Here are a few of the common concerns I've heard along the way, with some advice to offer comfort.

Senior Apartment Living

All my things won't fit!

How to handle: this will probably be true. You will need to discuss with them their preferences for their mementos and valuables. For more information, please see my explanations of 'The real meaning of value' at the start of Chapter 3. They need to feel comfortable with all of the decisions made, so be sure and discuss every possibility. If you are going to use a professional service, then reassure them that their needs and their possessions will be taken care of according to their plan. Assure them there will be no surprises.

This is not my home!

How to handle: this concern is a way of expressing their emotional connection to their family home. In this instance, it is best to listen with care. Your loved one needs your support to transition from the home they loved to their new living space. Focus on the positives, reminding them that the house they once lived in is no longer manageable or appropriate for them now. It is the best way to reassure them they have done the right thing; you understand their feelings and most importantly they will be taking all of their memories with them.

Relocation To A Family Member's Home Or The Granny Flat

I will just be in the way!

How to handle: this is entirely NOT true! Let them know that they are a welcome addition to your home and property. You are family, and family takes care of each another.

It's one of the wonderful joys of life. Have expectations in place about the roles people will take. You could even have an 'Expectation Contract' drawn up. This contract can cover chores along the lines of who mows the lawns and also how much babysitting is expected. Being able to repay those who helped you throughout your life is incredibly rewarding. You can let them be involved and feel useful in many ways. Organise some well-communicated tasks they feel comfortable with and capable of. It might include watering some plants, feeding the family pet or even making lunches for the kids. If you end up building a well designed Granny Flat, you may have far more privacy than you think.

You do things differently to me

How to handle: this is a valid concern. The truth is that living with new people or in a new living arrangement can be hard on everyone. Having a family meeting to discuss concerns is an excellent idea at this point. *Do you have teenage children who often stay up late and make noise?* You may need to implement a family code based on these changes. Be Courteous, Be Kind and Be Loving is my motto. Again, the Granny Flat option means your loved one will still be living independently with the same great community and neighbours, with far less stress.

Setting The Flight Plan – How And Where To Fly

The Decision To Sell / Rent Out / Build a Granny Flat
What's In It For Me?

According to Kotter, creating a sense of urgency (and understanding the truth about Rightsizing and why this is a good thing for you) underpins this project start-up. Hopefully, you are now feeling a little more motivated and excited about reading further.

The challenge is to complete Kotter's next step of 'powerful coalition' - finding your team. Don't underestimate the time and process involved in this project and give yourself the support you will need. Major change can feel like 'mission impossible' if you are attempting to do this on your own.

It is time to start organising a support team and communicating with the people around you. The team may be your local coffee shop owner, a neighbour, relatives or a business like mine. Again, a problem shared is a problem halved. Even if you're a tad undecided about your Rightsize, start talking about it and most importantly, see how you feel along the way.

Out of this entire process, the initial decision-making process is the hardest part. Once you believe in yourself and realise you are doing the right thing, the project becomes a logistical process. It can still be incredibly emotional. However, the feeling of being 'stuck' can shift.

We discussed the first part of the 'vision' with the bucket list exercise. Now we are going to get into 'financial matters' and work out if you are in a position to sell or rent out your existing home (and possibly build a Granny Flat) in this second part of your 'vision'. This section is about deciding what characteristics you would like in your new home. There should be a certain amount of 'non-negotiables' as well as considerations or 'meet-in-the-middle' requests. It is also critical to be thinking about what you would like your future lifestyle to look like. As soon as you free up some of your own hard-earned money, by Rightsizing you will be able to do some of the things you have dreamed about and enjoy this next stage of your life.

Following is a useful table you can photocopy so that you can create your next property 'wishlist'. This list will help you clarify your requirements and distinguish between your real needs and wants. Do this with your support team or life partner, if you have one, and listen to his or her requests or needs as well as prioritising your own. What may be important to him or her may not be as important to you. The happier he or she is with your next move, the more comfortable you both will be.

Take some time to consider how you can future-proof your next move, so it suits your lifestyle for many years to come. This wishlist helps crystalise your vision so that you become very clear about how you would like to spend the next stage of your retirement and the ideal environment in which you want to live.

By this stage of the book, you will have acknowledged your circumstance, made a decision to create change, shared your feelings with loved ones and understood the need to engage a support team. You will have also filled out your 'bucket list' and you are now about to fill out your 'property wishlist'.

Completing these tasks as we go along will help you feel like you are moving forward and that you can help make a huge difference. You will feel much clearer about where you are heading and even a little more positive about your next move. You will also feel more connected - or disconnected - to your partner. It may take time to both be on the same page. Hang in there. You are doing the right thing.

My Property Wishlist

Name:							
Budget:	Min: $			Max: $			
Preferred Suburbs:							
Property Type:	House	Townhouse	Terrace	Duplex	Apartment	Unit	
Bedrooms:							
Bathrooms:							
Car spaces (Garage):							
Condition of Property:	Brand New		Renovated		Unrenovated	Not Important	
Style:	(modern, heritage federation, architect design, etc)						

Copyright © 2020. Rightsize Your Home. All rights reserved.

My Property Wishlist

What is the most important criteria for you to purchase?

- [ ] Proximity to family / friends
- [ ] Walk the the shops, beach, cafés etc
- [ ] Transport links
- [ ] Level access (no stairs)
- [ ] Aspect
- [ ] Room for guests
- [ ] Storage Space
- [ ] Low maintenance Parking
- [ ] Visitors Parking
- [ ] Outdoor area
- [ ] Pet friendly
- [ ] Pool in complex
- [ ] Balcony
- [ ] Child friendly
- [ ] Quiet / Serene
- [ ] Good neighbours
- [ ] Views

Write your own criteria including must have's and desirable features:

Savings Basics

There are many immobilising factors when Rightsizing. A very common example is around financials. This can potentially inhibit the entire Downsizing process from even starting. Again, I believe the hardest part of the process is making the decision to Rightsize. Now, we are diving into the logistical side of the process which begins with understanding your financial situation.

The next step is to really understand your financial situation so that you feel more in control. Your future options will rely heavily on the right advice. It can make a huge impact on where you can go from here and how much money you are left with at the end of the day.

I strongly advise engaging a financial advisor who specialises in retirement. Your current accountant may not be aware of the benefits you can receive when Downsizing. Recently, the Australian Government has introduced incentives regarding superannuation and Downsizing. In Victoria, Pensioners can be exempt from stamp duty. You will need to understand the legislation so you can take advantage of these incentives. All of this can be explained to you by the right advisor.

If you have been working with an accountant up until now, getting some strategic financial advice that will be more relevant to the next stage of your life is imperative. Your advisor should be fully qualified and have a deep understanding of the financial and legal implications, as well as the 'ins' and 'outs' of Centrelink, pensions etc. Even if you think you don't need this advice, believe me, you do.

At a recent 'Downsizing Seminar' an attendee mentioned she was not aware she could get a tax exemption because she was a pensioner. She had already sold her home and Downsized. Unfortunately, she could not recoup any money she had paid and was extremely upset when she found out.

The Rightsizing process will help you leave no stone unturned. If you skip any of the steps, you may look back and wish you had done things differently, and we certainly do not want this to be the case.

What The Financial Experts Say

What we can tell you about money is that keeping a large family home is costing you an absolute fortune. At this stage of your life, you should not be worrying about bills, debts, home maintenance, or mortgages. Your health and happiness are of utmost importance.

If you are in a property that is approximately two-thirds larger than you need (ie. 4 or 5-bedroom home but you could quite comfortably survive in a 2 or 3-bedroom home), apart from all of the maintenance costs, think about these:

1. Consider the environment and the smaller bills

Keeping your 4 or 5-bedroom home cool during summer and warm during winter would mean a more significant electricity bill. You can save on utilities and your mortgage (if applicable) with a smaller house. Not only will this make your wallet smile. it will also help the environment as you will be consuming less energy. There is a great deal of discussion regarding the positive impact Rightsizing has on the environment. I can not agree more about this sentiment. Consider the footprint of unused space in an Empty Nester's home.

2. Savings, Savings, Savings!

Since you are possibly paying less for your new home, you may release equity which can boost your retirement savings. This will definitely boost your retirement savings. Now, you can use your savings on investments, enjoying your interests, or maybe even a trip to see your grandchildren.

3. Easy Maintenance

A smaller space will be easier to clean, with fewer bulbs to replace, fewer sheets to change, fewer windows to wash. This means that someone else can clean the pool (and get paid for it!). Your bills for hiring help with the cleaning, gardening or other home help areas will decrease.

As you now know, I meet most of my clients in the 'immobilised' section of change. So much so, in fact, I can see they have stayed in their large home for way too long. At one appraisal I was conducting for a local Real Estate Agent, I arrived at the property to see my 80+ year old client up a fully extended ladder on top of his cliffside property attempting to 'fix' his leaking roof, shuffling himself along on a piece of board suspended between the front doorway structure and side of the house!

Why? He didn't trust any trades or services to attend his property and didn't know how much he should pay for the service. He did not want to be 'ripped off' and so did not want to call for any help. Imagine the relief and happiness he would have had if he had Rightsized earlier!

Another client had also stayed in her property far too long. The neighbour of this lady hired me. The husband had ended up caring for his wife for many years. This property was up a steep driveway and had a stair chair inside. We had many years of belongings to work through and the home was enormous.

Of course, we got the job done successfully. We did a fantastic job but it was a real challenge, especially for the client.

If only this were all dealt with sooner. It just gives me so much pleasure when I meet people who are still in their early retirement and young enough to Rightsize and enjoy the benefits it brings. It is clear that they want to invest their money into creating a better future and lifestyle for themselves rather than into their 'time-and dollar-sucking' property.

Planning ahead and preparing yourself for the Rightsize just avoids all of these extreme circumstances, and your friends and family will love you more for it. If you do know anyone who needs help, please pass this book along after you finish it and they may be encouraged to Rightsize as well!

So let's plan ahead now and take a further look at your finances.

Working Out The Nest Finances

There is a lot of information that goes into deciding to Rightsize. Usually these decisions are finance-based, blended with some personal requirements about what you would like to happen with your home, and how you envisage your future.

Where Is Your Rightsized Home?

Are you thinking about a straight private purchase, retirement living, over 55s or building a Granny Flat?

Or Even A Sea Change / Tree Change Or Overseas Change?

In bedding down the property vision, it all starts by understanding the money side. It is never too late of course, but engaging a financial planner before you start is a great idea. With a planner's help, you can get a good idea of what you can afford to spend on your new home, moving in, all associated costs and what to do with any leftover funds.

To complete the 'where to buy' it must start with a ballpark figure of how much you think your property is worth. One value is as a rental income, and the other value is as a sale figure. This valuation will give you a starting point to work out what you can afford and where you stop. Therefore, you can work out and feel better about the whole project and start looking forward to where you think you're going to be.

In my business, we prepare the property for sale or rent depending on what the financial planner has worked out for the client. Australia has experienced an enormous number of changes in finance legislation recently. These changes mean some clients who previously thought of selling their house have found it more beneficial to create a rental income from their home.

On the other hand, a financial planner can also discuss various Granny Flat strategies with you. For example, where an Empty Nester builds a Granny Flat, rents it out for a while intending to eventually move into it themselves, while their family moves into the existing, more substantial property. They could also choose to rent it out for extra retirement income.

Changes in planning legislation regarding building Granny Flats has become easier and creating a Granny Flat is a valuable option to consider. There are circumstances where it is great for investment, for downsizing planning and the family.

Essentially, the project planning of a downsize remains the same for you, regardless of your next move. You will need to understand your financial situation, present your home for sale or rent, find a new home and then move into your new home.

To help navigate the options available of selling, renting or building a Granny Flat for Empty Nesters, II have asked my trusted friend and colleague, Jenny Simmonds, Certified Financial Planner (B.Sc, Dip SM, Adv Dip FS, CFP), to write this guest section in my book. Jenny and I have known each other for quite some time. We often work together looking after Empty Nester clients. Jenny has also shared helpful information at our Rightsizing Seminars. I love the message she shares about being prepared earlier and her quality understanding of Senior's finances.

Please note: Any general financial advice contained within this book does not consider your individual objectives, financial situation or needs ('Circumstances'). Nothing in this book is intended to be investment or personal financial advice or a recommendation to invest in a financial product. Before making any investment decision, you should consider the appropriateness of the information to your Circumstances and read any applicable Product Disclosure Statement ('PDS').

***

The Financial Need To 'Rightsize'

by Jenny Simmonds, Certified Financial Planner

I rarely see clients who are 'Rightsizing' for lifestyle reasons alone. Nearly all also have a financial need or desire to release some equity from their home, or generate more income to fund their retirement lifestyle, i.e. 'asset rich, income poor'.

The facts are these:

- Compulsory superannuation has not been around long enough to be able to adequately fund most people's retirement lifestyles, and
- Age pension is not generous enough to fund a comfortable retirement lifestyle on its own.

So unless;

1. there is a healthy inheritance coming your way,
2. you have been ploughing extra money into your superannuation above and beyond the mandatory employer contributions,
3. you intend to continue working throughout your retirement years,
4. you have other investments to draw on, or
5. you are hoping to win lotto...

...then it's likely that at some point in your retirement you will need to look to your largest financial asset, the family home, for a solution to meet your retirement lifestyle goals.

For many, a 'Rightsize' can't come soon enough. For others, there is great reluctance, and consequently a strong desire to put off any decision to sell or release equity from their family home for as long as possible, for one reason or another. Where this is the case, it is the financial planner's job to help you achieve this goal if possible. Or to outline the alternatives or financial trade-offs that may need to be made to help you stay in your family home for as long as desired.

When I see clients who are considering a 'Rightsize' they often have a common list of pressing financial questions they would like answered, such as:

1. *When is the best time to 'Rightsize' from a financial point of view?*
2. *How much equity will I need to release to meet my retirement lifestyle goals?*
3. *How much will this leave me with to spend on a new home?*
4. *What options to buy does this leave me with?*
5. *What will I do with the remaining proceeds?*
6. *How long can I expect these proceeds to last?*
7. *What sort of income will this provide me with?*
8. *How do these impact my age pension entitlements?*
9. *What are my alternatives?*

What Does A Financial Planner Do?

In summary, it is a financial planner's job to:

1) Help you identify your financial needs, goals and objectives.

2) Educate you on the various strategies, investment options and product types available to establish which are going to meet your needs.

3) Make any recommendations that are in your best interest to meet your goals, needs and objectives, as best as possible; and

4) Partner with you over the long term to monitor and review how you and your investments are tracking to plan and make any adjustments (as needed) along the way as things change.

To be able to answer the questions listed above, a financial planner will need to get to know you and your financial position. He or she will try to find out what lifestyle goals are important to you, as each generally translate to financial planning considerations. You will need to be prepared to be open about your situation and goals as much as you can be. I often find that clients become more aware of their major financial goals through this defining process, and this increased awareness provides them with greater clarity and confidence about their financial future.

In getting to know you and identifying your needs, goals and objectives, the planner will want to discuss several key areas.

Cost Of Living

One of the primary needs to be identified is how much regular income you need to comfortably meet your regular costs of living. This varies from person to person and couple to couple, and there are no golden rules here; everyone spends differently.

As a guide to 'comfortable', I usually define this as enough to

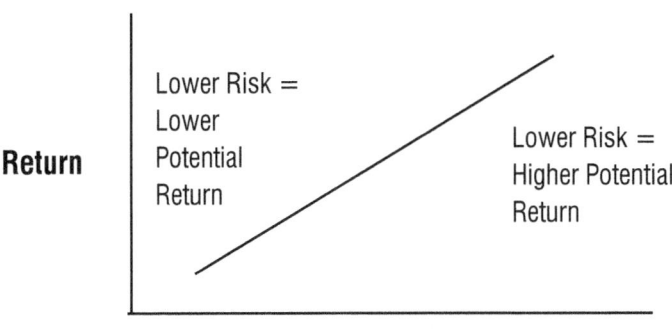

not have to think twice about ordering a cup of coffee when you are out, but still being aware of your spending habits. It also usually covers a couple of weekends away and a short domestic holiday each year, but not your big-ticket one-off expenses, such as international holidays or a new car.

A good start is to sit down and use a budget planner to identify how much you currently need to meet your regular expenses. Try to be as realistic as possible with your expenses and once you've done your budget, follow it up with a reality test: i.e. how much net income are you currently receiving and how much of this are you actually saving? Is there a gap between your budget and what you've been spending?

Next you need to consider how your expenses are likely to change going forward, if at all.

For example:
- *Are you going to be driving less and therefore spending less on fuel?*
- *Are you going to be eating out more or less?*

- *Are you going to be playing more golf?*
- *Perhaps you will no longer have to pay for lawn mowing, but you may have to pay strata levies.*

As a guide, the Association of Superannuation Funds of Australia (ASFA) does a quarterly survey to benchmark the annual budget needed by retired Australians to fund their retirement. Their findings as at the end of December 2019, are that a couple looking to achieve a comfortable retirement will need to budget for $62,269 a year, while a single person would need to budget for $44,146. A couple looking to fund a modest retirement will need to budget for $40,560 a year, while a single person will need to budget for $28,165.

Big Ticket Expenses

It is also important to define any potential big-ticket expenses, such as:

- *When will your car next need updating?*

- *Are you planning any large holidays? If so, how many, how often and in what time frame?*

- *Have you planned to make any gifts or commitments to assist your loved ones, e.g. weddings, grandchildren's education costs, financial dependents?*

- *Do you have any debts or credit card balances outstanding?*

What Sort Of Investor Are You?

When I ask this question, most people will automatically

describe themselves as 'conservative', but I often then pick up their superannuation statement to find that they have been investing in the default investment option within their fund, with 70%- 80% exposure to shares and property for the last 15 years! This is not a conservative investment option. Again, everyone is different and has different tolerances to volatility.

The key is to establish:

- Your 'sleep at night' threshold, i.e. what level of volatility you can tolerate, allowing your money to work as hard as possible without keeping you awake at night with worry.
- What is your understanding of investment markets?
- What do you need your investments to earn on average to meet your goals?
- How long do you have to invest?

When it comes to how to invest, it is important that your planner outlines how different investments work, the relationship between risk and return and the importance of diversification (i.e. not having 'all your eggs in the one basket'). There is often quite an education process required before defining a client's risk profile.

What Else Is Important To You When It Comes To Money?

Then there are the multitude of other financial considerations and attitudes that are unique to each of us, such as:

- *"I don't ever want to have to pay tax again."*
- *"I have paid taxes all my life, so now I want to ensure that I*

receive as much age pension as possible". Or occasionally it is the opposite, "I've never had to rely on government support before and don't want to start now."

- "I am happy to see my retirement savings deplete over time to fund my retirement, but want to make sure that at least my family home is left to my children when I pass away." Or "I have spent most of my life looking after my children. This is my turn now and I've told them when I'm gone they'll be lucky if there's a dollar left!"

Meeting Goals And Setting Expectations

As part of the planning process, it is important that the planner looks holistically at their client's situation, including:

- How a client's income needs will keep pace with inflation.
- How to maximise age pension (assuming this is a goal of the client).
- Ensuring any released capital is enough to meet retirement lifestyle needs beyond life expectancy (as 50% of us exceed our life expectancy) or, alternatively, that the client is fully aware that further equity may need to be released in the future.
- Are unexpected expenses catered for?
- Are the client's estate planning goals catered for and necessary documents in place?
- Are future planned expenses catered for?
- What will happen if investment returns end up being less than expected?

Client's expectations need to be set and, where necessary, adjusted or re-set to ensure that goals are realistic and disappointments minimised.

How To Choose A Financial Planner?

ASIC offers some great tips on how to pick a financial planner and what questions to ask/what to expect on its Money Smart website: www.moneysmart.gov.au/investing/financial-advice.

If you are choosing a financial planner, my suggestion would be to meet with at least two and ask yourself the following questions:

1) Are they qualified and licensed to provide financial advice?

2) Do you feel comfortable with them?

3) Do you feel at ease to ask any questions you may have?

4) Do you feel they have listened to you and understood your needs, goals and objectives?

5) Have they been clear on their fees and what they can do for you?

6) Have they discussed putting any specific recommendations in writing for you prior to proceeding with any recommendations?

When To See A Financial Planner?

As early as possible in the process. I often see clients several years earlier so that expectations are set, and they have a plan in place for their future. The earlier you receive financial advice the more empowered and confident you will feel about your financial future. Ideally, the relationship will commence from when you first have your own financial goal!

When 'Rightsizing' is imminent, I will often see my clients several times over a short period as it's 'crunch time' and final decisions are being made. Your planner should work closely with you and your team to ensure that the process is as stress-free and enjoyable as possible.

"Rightsizing" Financial Planning Considerations And Tips

Buying Before You Sell

The thought of waiting to sell your home before buying your new one is one of the most common concerns I come across with 'Rightsizers'. *"What if I can't find a new home in time and end up having to rent, resulting in two moves?"* Or, *"I don't want to feel pressured to buy my new home quickly."*

While these are valid concerns and, yes, there is a chance that you may have to move twice, there are often greater financial risks associated with 'buying before you sell', including:

- The pressure to sell your existing home quickly and therefore the risk of accepting a lower price, leaving you ultimately out of pocket.

- The possibility that you have to fund expensive bridging finance while waiting for your existing house to sell, which may take much longer than expected.

Although both options contain unknowns and risks, unless you have the available cash to afford your new home sitting in the bank, it is usually a financially safer option to 'sell before you buy'.

While I have come across a number of financial disasters for clients who have bought before they have sold, I can't recall any from clients who have sold before they bought. The most common outcome is that they find the perfect house in time to arrange settlement for the new purchase on the same day as the sale of their existing house, moving straight from one house into the other.

My tip is to be prepared for the possibility that you will have to put your home contents into storage and move somewhere temporarily in between selling and buying, whether it be a friend or relative's house, house sitting, arranging an extended booking at a caravan park or a holiday house or serviced apartments. As Belinda will cover, it does not matter that you don't know exactly where you will Rightsize to. Don't forget that if it does eventuate that you will have to move twice, that you will have the advantage of interest/income on your existing house sale proceeds being available to you to help with any accommodation and storage costs. And Centrelink offers concessions on any amounts invested that are intended to be used for the new house purchase for up to 12 months while in between home purchases.

Are You Considering A Retirement Village?

A villa in a retirement village can often offer desirable retirement lifestyle features, such as security, social interaction, services and facilities as a retirement accommodation option. The contractual arrangements for entry into retirement village accommodation come in many different forms and a complete understanding of your legal entitlements are of fundamental importance.

Most will require an 'entry contribution' and ongoing levies to be paid and then there are deferred acquisition costs that will be deducted from the entry contribution upon leaving the village. Most provide services as part of the levies with additional services available at an additional cost. Often the contractual arrangements are what are commonly termed a '99-year lease', whereas others will offer a strata title ownership. <u>It is important to understand the difference and whether your ownership will allow you be entitled to a share of any capital gain in the villa value or not.</u>

Having a legal practitioner look over the contract is highly recommended. A financial planner should be able to look at affordability and strategies as well as government entitlements.

Tip: *Did you know that in some cases (depending on the amount of entry contribution paid) age pensioners who enter a retirement village may also receive rent assistance?*

Granny Flats or Multi-Generational Living

With affordable housing being limited in Australia, especially in major capital cities like Sydney, there is a marked increase in Granny Flat construction and multi-generational living arrangements. Belinda again will discuss this option some more as you read on. These can come in many forms, including:

- Selling and moving into a loved one's home where a Granny Flat has been built (whether internally attached to the house or in the backyard).

- Loved ones moving into your home into separate self-contained accommodation (whether internally attached to the house or in the backyard).
- Selling your home and purchasing a new home together with loved ones with separate self-contained accommodation available or created.
- Constructing a Granny Flat in your home (whether internally attached to the house or in the backyard) and renting it out to provide extra disposable income, or renting out your oversized family home and you living in the new Granny Flat.

When private arrangements are made with loved ones they are often mutually satisfying, for example releasing capital for the retiree to live on and providing affordable housing for loved ones that may otherwise not be accessible or limited. There may also be other motivating factors, understandings or agreements behind such arrangements. These range from financial arrangements through to agreements relating to the level of care for the retiree that may be provided now or in the future, garden and property maintenance or child care. It is important that all parties are clear on expectations and these are all well documented.

My tips here are as follows:

- *Make sure you receive financial advice early in the planning process. In particular, there are many implications for age pension entitlements, especially as they relate to the Gifting rules where assets are transferred to loved ones in exchange for a life interest in a home or care to be provided,*
- *When arrangements are entered into with loved ones make sure all financial, care and lifestyle expectations are clearly*

communicated and understood between loved ones from the onset, including any immediate family (eg siblings) that may not be directly involved in the living arrangements (where appropriate). These include details such as the splitting of bills, maintenance of the property and lawns, expectations for level of care or babysitting, break conditions (e.g. notice requirements if one party wants to sell or if there is a relationship breakdown). I have seen some great contracts that include dispute resolution procedures and measures to ensure each party continues to respect the privacy needs of the others. Hopefully these measures won't need to be utilised, however disputes and relationship breakdowns do occur and including such measures can help prevent disputes from getting out of hand.

- Make sure you seek legal advice regarding the documentation of these expectations / agreements as well as about the legal ownership of the property (e.g. tenants in common and in what proportions).

Relocating – Trying Before You Buy

If you intend to relocate, moving to a new area is a very big decision and, like all things, requires careful consideration and research. It takes time to discover whether a new location is going to suit you or not. There will be varying access to infrastructure including hospital and medical resources, shops and restaurants. There are also the social considerations. It can be a very expensive mistake to relocate to an area that you later discover you don't like or perhaps just doesn't feel right.

My tip is to take a few holidays in your short-listed area(s), or even better consider renting in the area for a while before you decide to sell and purchase. Some of my clients have rented out the family home for a while and rented where they think they would like to live before selling and purchasing. Preparing your home to rent out can also reduce the load for preparing the home to sell down the track!

New 'Downsizer's' Superannuation Contributions

From 1/7/2018, new legislation came into effect allowing downsizers who have lived in their family home for at least 10 years, and are aged 65 and over, to be able to add up to $300,000 each (nb: maximum $600,000 per couple) of their house sale proceeds to superannuation, without having to meet a work test.

This exciting new provision opens up flexible and tax effective investment opportunities for downsizers that were not previously available.

Tip: *Please make sure you seek financial advice early regarding this provision if you feel it applies to you, to ensure you get the timing right and make the most out of the benefits of this new opportunity.*

Celebrating The Decision To Go
Continuing with Belinda Woolrych

After having a fresh financial model in place, the decision to Rightsize can then be crystallised. I have seen many tears at the signature stage. It's important to remember that we are only human and it's okay to have mixed emotions. It's not unusual to feel guilt or loss and even trauma at this time.

On the other hand, I have seen couples so excited about the release from their property, there are plenty of celebratory champagnes and a great amount of enthusiasm. I'm proud to say our staff have received the same level of thanks and praise for playing our part in making the project happen.

Whether it is sadness or joy, it is important to acknowledge the feeling of loss, grief or release as part of a very important milestone in the change process.

I'd like to tell you why I feel so positive about people making this decision. I want to help you understand how it feels for some of my clients and how they have dealt with others coming into their long-loved home.

Like all relationships, some break ups can be positive and refreshing and others not so. Essentially, it's the same here. There is a 'break up' of a partnership and, quite literally, the walls of a family home can feel very memorable and personal. Home has been a place where you have experienced so much of life and it deserves a major celebration. When you Rightsize, it deserves to be marked with a celebratory event. Making this event a milestone is critical to Kotter's theory and to a successful change transition; unfreeze the norm, and re-freeze in a new form.

After you have thoroughly revised your financials, a decision is made about whether to sell, rent out or rent out, and build a Granny Flat at your home. Herein lies the need for celebration: permanent change is about to occur and paying homage to your feelings needs to be addressed.

I have a number of suggestions regarding how you can create and commemorate this milestone to assist with moving forward. Again, you don't need to know exactly where or when you are going, it is the placing of a 'stake in the ground'. It is the decision that is to be celebrated.

Your 'to do' list for this milestone is as follows:

1. Make it clear to your friends and family that you have decided to move.
2. Verbalise it to yourselves and your inner circle.
3. Create a photo book of your home and make enough copies for your children and any special people in your life, just the way it is.
4. Have a real celebration and invite your inner circle, special friends and family to attend a 'leaving home for a Rightsize' party.
5. Make a date and roster all your decluttering program times.
6. Make a date for your friends/family to come and pick up all their belongings, or get them to arrange a courier to deliver it to them.
7. Conduct an Initial Appraisal to plan your property presentation.
8. Make a future date for your move.
9. Make superb plans on your bucket list.
10. Understand that your new property is going to be amazing, with only the items that you really love making it there.

Real Estate Then, Real Estate Now

Just think how often things have seriously changed in our lives. The incredible fact is that, whether you are renting or buying, more than 80% of potential buyers are now researching from their mobile devices.

Even desktop computers are Rightsizing, and the numbers of mobile devices are increasing. Desktop computers have had their spike and are more unpopular now than they ever were (some countries have skipped the entire desktop generation and have just gone mobile!). Therefore, appealing to your property buying target market means some non-negotiables will get you a better result financially, as well as helping you save time.

Your property must offer what the target market is looking for and look great for your professional real estate photography. With your property presentation done well, your buyers will come, and it probably won't be from seeing your home in a real estate office front window. Their 'windows' will be located on the internet, through their mini-computers - their mobile devices.

The real estate experience can be an overwhelming one. Ask any real estate agent who is a Baby Boomer about the difference over the years. They have had to cope with hundreds of their tasks changing over the years. There is no doubt, the real estate industry itself has experienced more change than any other.

The sale and rental process is happening at the speed of light. Agents are now running their business from the 'virtual' office; their mobile devices. They can tap into thousands of purchasers, fantastic property history and they can profile your suburb and your competition in minutes.

A buyer can now hold their mobile device up to a property, scan and an application will feed back all sorts of information about the property in no time. The buyer can find out more about your property in a matter of seconds than you may know yourself as the owner. Incredible!

A significant number of my clients have not experienced a property sale for anywhere up to 15-50 years. A client I saw recently, for an Initial Appraisal, was my longest standing homeowner of 54 years and her mother was born in the home!

Our typical Empty Nesters' properties are often the original builder/purchasers from the first 1960's and 70's suburb releases. Our other type of typical property owner is the second cycle of the family generation now living in the Empty Nest.

Whatever the type of property or its location, the issues and challenges are still the same for the vendor (or purchaser). We have completed many makeovers for this era of property, and there are common solutions. The building style and property layout can be quite typical of that era and, in fact, the décor is quite typical of that era, too. Combine this with the expectations of the contemporary market and the solutions are also often quite the norm.

Our owners in the 60's suburbs were often the builders or supervised the build and ensured the property was laid out to their particular need at the time of building. The purpose-built house had a typical layout and was often built by young couple new Homeowners, considering having or with young children. These children stayed through the period of primary and high school and then have typically stayed on while at university, or gone to travel or have their own family, and then the cycle begins again. This very 'cycle beginning again' individual is your target market and your most likely purchaser.

These purchasers are families with changed needs and now desire your traditional property space. In the 'Nest Makeover' chapter ahead, I'll be sharing some of my secrets about what your potential purchasers or tenants are looking for and how to go about appealing to them. The reason you need to do this is so you can generate the best possible outcome, being more income for you and a better settlement period - whatever makes it easier for your transition.

However, for now, we're looking at the real estate process and the way your target market is searching for properties. Here is an interesting scenario about your most likely target market that will want to purchase or rent your home:

They are working and usually very busy professionals and may or may not have children as yet. They are purchasing for their future which will most likely be to raise a family. Their reasons will primarily be the same as yours, when you first bought your home. With any luck, they will raise their family in your home and love it as much as you do.

There is also the possibility a developer will buy your home and knock it down. However, by making your home look at its most appealing in a cost-effective manner, you are creating competition and it is more likely a young family will fall in love with your home and buy from an emotional perspective, beating the developer to it!

If the price is within their desired budget, your purchaser or target could be coming from out of the area, or indeed they could be local (all properties are open to anyone now with the digital age and speed of searching).

First, they will search, usually by the number of bedrooms and location. They will then compare price points. They will view your property via the two main internet portals for home sales at realestate.com.au or domain.com.au (probably while cooking dinner and doing an online grocery shop at the same time), checking other details along with your electronic floor plan.

Your target has started with an internet hit of many thousands of properties, they have filtered it down to hundreds, they have narrowed again by viewing a satellite image on 'Google Earth' and 'Street View' and have looked through the street in a virtual walk-through, cutting down again on photos that are not looking contemporary enough. Your target has filtered again by the requirements. Now they are down to a short list of possible viewings.

Now, the street stalking starts! Your target has sent their Aunt, Gran, and Sister down to have a look to find out what they think. *Can you see how hard your property has had to work to even get a 'look in' against your competition?*

This busy target now has a full Saturday of possible viewings listed in her electronic diary, starting at 10am, then 10.30am, 11.15am, 12pm - and it goes on and on. So if there is something that puts them off as they drive up to your property, or they say, 'Oh, we'll look next week,' then chances are you'll never see them again!

In summary, your target is typically digitally savvy and busy, so you need to listen and understand these contemporary expectations to create an effective marketing campaign - and make sure your home creates an unforgettable impression, the very first time it is viewed.

How Do You Cope With The Thought Of Others Living In Your Nest?

When it comes time to rent or sell your property, you will need to hire a professional. The last thing you should be doing is selling or renting out a property yourself. I can't stress this highly enough.

I have an investment property and have bought and sold a few times. At no time have I ever considered or wanted to do this myself. Unless you are a fully licensed property manager or Real Estate Agent, you know the current property market backward and have sharp negotiation skills, don't even think about it.

To get the job done, you will also need to be unbiased and emotionally unattached to your property; and to date I have not met one Rightsizer who meets all of the said requirements.

Selling, as opposed to leasing your property, will undoubtedly be the most emotionally challenging changeover for you. I hear my clients talk about the horror of thinking someone will knock down their home, or change all the things they loved about their home. In many cases, my clients have built their own homes, and the thought of someone 'destroying' them is devastating.

A sense of complete ownership due to the length of time spent at your property will trigger these thoughts. I also believe that following the 'milestone celebration steps' will ensure your current memories are treasured and captured. This is critical for you to release the property in your mind to the envisaged new owners and allow them to enjoy their family's upbringing there.

Understanding your home may need a significant re-design, or just a tweak to appeal to your target market now and adequately preparing your home will see you are rewarded for your efforts financially.

You are freeing up a lovely family space for a young couple to move into and make their own, just like you did when you purchased it. If the purchaser happens to be an investor or someone wanting to rebuild, my suggestion is 'don't look back'! Just prepare the property well and enjoy the financial benefits it will bring.

Savour your memories and after you have made your decision to move and have celebrated that, it is best to treat the entire property changeover as a business transaction.

If you have made your property as appealing as possible and you have attracted the broadest amount of potential purchasers, then you have done your job. You will be able to realise the profit and secure a fantastic future in a more appropriate sized home. You should not feel worried about the property and what happens to it after you sell - it should not matter to you.

If you find you do worry about your home after it is sold, or rented out, revisit the reasons why you have made the change. Talk about your concerns with family and friends and your support crew. Do not ignore your feelings. Try your best to turn them around by accepting life is full of changes and this is a crucial one, for your ultimate health and happiness.

If you want to achieve the best possible rental return, then just like going for the best sale return you may need to undertake some maintenance or renovations from a legal perspective, before you can advertise your property.

Chances are you are appealing to a tenant that was probably a similar profile to you when you bought the property. Again, this person may be 30 years younger than you and will lead quite a different life. There are things they will request and you will still need to pay for them, like a good dishwasher!

Discussions with Property Makeover Specialists (like us) and a Financial Planner at this stage will be helpful. You may be able to make the necessary changes before tenancy and other requests that can commence once you have rented it out for a while.

Please be aware that renovations for tenancy have specific rules and regulations from a tax point of view, and the spend v's return should be carefully scrutinised. Your property should also be reviewed every year, according to the current market, and the updates to your property should see an increase in your rental return. Again, working with a Property Makeover Specialist to work out what needs to be done would be highly recommended.

Outsourcing To A Buyers' Agent

Rich Harvey, CEO & Founder, Buyers' Agent www.propertybuyer.com.au

If you have not purchased a home in the past 10 or 20 years, then you will discover the whole process of buying and selling has changed significantly and can appear daunting. But don't be dismayed or put off – help is readily at hand. A professional 'Buyers' Agent' will work with you each step of the way to ensure a smooth transition, and to help you find your new home that will meet as many of your 'wishes' as possible. A professional Buyers' Agent works exclusively for you, the buyer, in helping you identify the right suburbs and properties to consider. The Buyers' Agent researches the property market and shortlists only those properties that meet your requirements – so you don't need to spend weekend upon weekend out amongst the crowds at open for inspections. Getting independent and trustworthy property advice is critical in the downsizing process. Sure the buyers agent charges a fixed fee- but they are typically able to save you far more than they charge by negotiating well and removing the stress and time consuming process of finding your next home.

The key difference between a Buyers' Agent and a traditional selling agent is who they represent. A Buyers' Agent works exclusively for the buyer, whereas the selling agent works for the vendor (seller). A Buyers' Agent charges for their service as either a fixed fee or as a percentage of the purchase price. A Buyers' Agent does not sell real estate. By law, an agent cannot act for (and accept a commission) from both parties in the transaction.

You will notice how intent each agent that pitches to sell your property is on getting the 'highest' price possible. Operating in this manner is great for the vendor but can end up costing the buyer more than they need to pay if the agent is a sharp negotiator.

A Buyers' Agent will take the stress and frustration out of the buying process. They will also ensure you are not paying too much for your next property and manage negotiations on your behalf. The property market is continually changing with the economic cycles, and the methods of sales and marketing are evolving, so it pays to get independent advice from someone that has your best interests at heart.

How Does A Buyers' Agent Work?

There are five main steps in the process:

1. **Create a Buyer Wishlist** – Starting with your needs, specific requirements, budget, suburb preferences and style, the Buyers' Agent creates a clear 'buyer's brief ' to commence searching. The Buyers' Agent can give you valuable insights

into the local market and help pinpoint the best value for money and lifestyle choices. They will help you future-proof your move by asking questions about what is most important to you and consider distance to shops, public transport, doctors and other amenities.

2. **Research and Shortlist** – Using an extensive network of agents and contacts, the Buyers' Agent searches the market and refines their selection of properties into a shortlist for your inspection. You inspect the properties at a convenient time with them and provide feedback on their suitability.

3. **Appraisal** – Once you have found a property that is ideal and you are happy to move forward, the Buyers' Agent prepares a written appraisal of the property using comparable sales to show its current market value. Property values are constantly adjusting to market conditions, so having an independent appraisal from a buyers agent means you are making a wise decision on price.

4. **Due Diligence** – The Buyers' Agent coordinates the pest and building inspections (or strata search if an apartment) to identify if there are any major concerns with the property. They also check the council records for any proposed neighbouring development applications that may impact the chosen property.

5. **Negotiate and Secure** – A professional Buyers' Agent will secure the property for the lowest possible price using their expert negotiation skills. They will protect you from making an emotional purchase and the intensive selling tactics often used by agents to bid buyers up. They'll bid for you at auction and negotiate for you in private treaty sales. They know the tricks of the trade and which moves to make at auction to be

successful. The Buyers' Agent will also facilitate the exchange of contracts and coordinate with your solicitor, saving you lots of stress running around.

Remember, the selling agent is not working for you in the real estate negotiation – they are working for the vendor. An independent Buyers' Agent will work with your best interests at heart to take a firm but fair approach to negotiating the best outcome for you. The Buyers' Agent provides a buffer of protection between you and the sales agent, so you don't end up paying too much.

One of the most significant benefits of using a Buyers' Agent is gaining access to their network and their knowledge. Finding 'just the right place' takes most buyers at least 6 to 12 months of hard and arduous research – calling agents, doing inspections and scouring the internet. A good Buyers' Agent has a large network of agents at their fingertips to call and find properties listed both on and off-market. These off-market deals are sometimes called "silent sales," and we regularly come across these opportunities. So a Buyer's Agent can give you access to a much broader variety and pool of properties than you may see on the internet. We typically find good properties within 30 to 60 days!

Another key benefit of using a Buyers' Agent is their ability to act quickly when a good property comes up for sale. In the current market, it is very competitive and buyers have to be prepared to move very fast to secure a property. If you have been out of the market for a long time, then it can take several months to get up to speed on pricing. As buying any property is a costly exercise, it can be great to get independent advice from a Buyers' Agent that gives accurate and timely appraisals. In summary, a Buyers' Agent will save you time, money and stress and be your key to making smarter buying decisions.

As a special bonus for 'Rightsize Your Home' readers, Propertybuyer has agreed to offer five special free downloads. Just visit: www.propertybuyer.com.au/resources/free-downloads to gain access to:

1. The Top Ten Classic Mistakes Property Buyers Make
2. Moving House Checklist
3. Property Inspection Checklist
4. How To Select Your Buyers Agent
5. How To Buy Off Market Properties

We hope your journey to your next property is a fun and exciting change for you.

***

What Are My Next Home Options?
Continuing with Belinda Woolrych

You have decided to Rightsize and now it is time to make a decision on where you will be happiest. The options available can be somewhat overwhelming. You will soon discover that there are both benefits and drawbacks with all of your options.

Following, you will find a small description of the scenarios you may have in mind. I will discuss some of the pros and cons as well as share some feedback from Empty Nesters who have experienced or who are currently experiencing the move.

Rightsizing To A Different Sized Private Home

Private home ownership, whether it be small or the same size with less maintenance, is something we are all familiar with. It is a traditional and independent property purchase. If you choose to purchase a home in this manner, you may opt for the same size home to still accommodate visiting family members. However, you may like to choose a property with less land or that will require less maintenance. For example, your new home may be situated on a flat block of land with no stairs or upper levels. Adjusting your home in this manner to suit your lifestyle is going to be a worthwhile decision, especially if made sooner rather than later. Rightsizing does not always mean downsizing.

This is often referred to as a 2-step downsize. The property may not suit you in the next 10-15 years. However, for now, it is the perfect option and one that you feel comfortable with. Decluttering and making sure you get rid of your excess belongings is highly recommended, even if most of it will fit in your new space.

I have a client we have previously worked with whose story made headlines in our local newspaper. 'Rightsizing is a hot topic', they said… 'we know!'. Here is a copy of the article, which I trust you will find interesting reading.

Manly Daily

The new buzz word for baby boomers buying property is not downsizing but 'rightsizing' as they often purchase something bigger, better and with less maintenance stress than their old home, **Kathryn Welling reports.** *Baby boomers born between 1946 and 1964 are a huge demographic in the peninsula property market. They are in the process of retiring and buying possibly their last home. Developers courting their custom have discovered something* *interesting: post-war boomers don't always want a retirement village and are 'downsizing' less and 'rightsizing' more.*

Downsizing expert Belinda Woolrych said the assumption that retirees want something smaller is not always correct. Often they just want less maintenance, room for the grand children, somewhere to entertain outside and something special such as a view or proximity to a cafe. "Ultimately, the next move in life isn't about downsizing or upsizing: It's about rightsizing. It's about ensuring less stress and a property that suits your needs," she said.

Over 55's Private Accommodation

These are buildings that have been designed to accommodate the 55+ age group. They are not only low maintenance, but they are also instantly suitable on a community level due to the specified demographic who are offered these homes to purchase. These homes are classed as a private purchase, without the additional features of a retirement village.

Some people choose to sell their home and Rightsize by buying a unit or apartment. These options are usually a strata title arrangement. A strata title is a certificate of title for a lot that also includes a share in the common property in a strata scheme set up and governed by an act which will specify the particulars. The strata scheme dictates what you own when you buy a strata titled lot and what is called 'common property'. There are many combinations of individual ownership and shared property.

Some examples are:

- Individual ownership of the buildings and areas inside and outside the premises;
- Individual ownership of inside and outside areas, but only

part of the building, e.g. the walls, but not the roof; and
- Ownership of inside and outside areas, but not any part of the building.

Depending on the strata scheme, the 'common property' may include exterior walls, courtyards, roofs and driveways, as well as shared facilities such as laundries, swimming pools, stairwells and lifts.

Before buying a strata-titled property, see a copy of the strata plan to check what you will own and what is 'common property'. This can be determined by viewing the ground floor page of the strata plan. Under regulations, some strata-titled schemes may be restricted to occupation by retired persons and their partners. A 'retired person' is defined as someone who is 55 years and over, or someone retired from full-time employment.

Source: www.commerce.wa.gov.au/consumerprotection/PDF/Publications/SeniorsHousingGuide.pdf

Retirement Living

Is retirement village living the right choice for you? I am sure this is something you may have considered. There are advertisements for retirement living in every newspaper you read.

Community living has many health and social benefits, and many of my clients are very happy enjoying the benefits living in a communal setting can bring. Make the time to visit a few in your local area and understand what they have to offer as well as their costs.

My suggestion would be not to leave this until it's too late. Moving to a retirement village is primarily a lifestyle decision, so it doesn't make sense to put it off until your health deteriorates.

It is not about that! Retirement Villages are a safe community with similarly aged residents and can offer some excellent advantages.

We recommend you visit and experience it first hand. Look at the unit options available and observe the village and the surrounding area in detail. It may take a few visits until you feel completely comfortable. Talk to village management and current residents. In particular, members of the Residents' Committee. The Retirement Village Handbook has extensive checklists and information you can work through.

Think ahead, as with any Rightsizing move, not just about the Retirement Village. Satisfy yourself that the village will be able to efficiently meet your needs in the future if you require additional assistance as you age.

What sort of facilities are available there, and will it suit you in the years to come? After this move, you may not be keen to do it all again!

This move, if you are getting on, would be your 1-step downsize. If you can see you will need some additional care in the near future, preferably make sure there are options available so you will not have to relocate again.

Understand the implications and issues raised by the different legal structures. Different legal structures have different effects and raise various issues regarding applicable legislation, stamp duty, GST, service charges and levies, responsibility for refurbishment and capital replacement costs, security of tenure, operator default, termination, vacating the premises, capital losses and credit risk. Again, the Retirement Village Handbook can be particularly useful, however we would suggest you seek professional advice.

Understand the fees. Work out how much the fees would be in a range of scenarios and satisfy yourself that it is suitable for your intended or likely period of occupation. Remember you will need advice on all of the fees.

It is best not to make decisions based solely on the initial entry price, capital gains, or the service charges or the departure fee structure. Retirement villages offer a range of benefits and involve a number of costs and risks, all of which should be taken into consideration.

Shop around. It's a good idea to look at several retirement villages before you make a final decision. You will then have at least some basis for comparison, which is usually the best way to identify value for money. Be aware that the variety of different legal structures and departure fee structures can make it very difficult to easily compare different villages. The Retirement Village Handbook can be particularly useful in this regard because it develops a methodology for comparing different villages on an 'apples and apples' basis.

Read the documentation and find a lawyer with retirement village experience. You should receive a pile of disclosure material and legal documentation. Read it, and don't rely on anything that's not in writing. Give a copy to your lawyer. Retirement villages are a complicated and specialised area of law, so it makes good sense to use a lawyer that has suitable experience and doesn't have to muddle through or reinvent the wheel.

Don't forget the big picture. Always remember that as well as a home, you need money to live on. Put a financial plan in place that will ensure you can have your cake and eat it, too. If you don't have a will or it no longer reflects your wishes, it is time to make one or have it updated.

Interstate / Sea Change / Tree Change / Overseas Change Short & Long Term Property Rental

If you are considering a move away from your current local area to an unknown area, you will first need to weigh up the pros and cons.

Even though it can be tempting to move somewhere that may be significantly cheaper to live to save money when buying back into the market; you will have to give this serious thought. You may be sacrificing your link to the community and your connection with family, and this is something you will miss the most.

I hear some extremely positive stories about successful big moves; however, I also listen to stories of where a move for all of the wrong reasons has not worked out well.

We had a scenario where a client moved to the NSW Central Coast and loved it. They are now living near their children and grand-children, close to shops and medical support for future needs - so it has worked out flawlessly. On the other hand, I have heard stories of people who have chosen to move to an area they didn't know and hated it. Unfortunately, they subsequently could not then go back for financial reasons.

Like everything, do your homework. A great idea would be to rent in an area for a while to learn about the community and see how you feel. You may even find an appropriate Airbnb property that suits you and is already furnished.

You can put a short-term lease on your existing property and go and try a few different areas that are on your list. In this way, you will still have your asset and can sell more confidently when you know where you are going when it settles. If you 'present' it correctly, you will attract premium rental while you are working things out.

I have clients that had us present their property immaculately for holiday rental and, as a result, have commanded a high return. They now choose to live half of the year away and half of the year in their home. What a fantastic idea!

Again, think ahead; what kind of support do you have now and what kind of support will you need in future years to come?

What home or area will suit you best?

Is it the right decision to make now and will it still be right for you over the coming years as well?

The Granny Flat

It is not uncommon to hear about of or see a Granny (or Glammy) Flat at a family home. This kind of solution may be perfect for you! You could possibly have one of these built at your property while you are still working and enjoy the income.

By building a Granny Flat, you will still have the same neighbours and community as well as your asset. If you plan on leasing, your property will no longer be your responsibility. Your property manager will maintain and handle your property (and also take care of the bills and hassles!).

In the design and planning stage there will be much to consider. For example, the design needs to ensure all future uses of the accommodation are to be considered in the structure. Illustrations of future-proofing design could be things like including a second bedroom in which grandchildren or a future in-home carer may need to stay. You may also need to consider wider hallways, a low side bath, more open plan, easier open shower access, reinforcements ready within walls for handles, easy taps and window locks. All of this is possible while maintaining a sleek and contemporary look. We have managed Granny Flat constructions and have implemented some stylish solutions for our happy clients. All of our designs have long term value-add in mind, carefully ensuring future target markets and family homes are not compromised.

Understanding if this could be an option for you is simple. You start by having your land checked for initial suitability, then go to the next stage of a site visit if given the go ahead. This initial land check is not too costly. It will consist of a standard checklist filled out by a professional and will means test all of the current requirements including block size and the Government requirements.

I believe this is such a great solution; I have built Granny Flats at my properties. The buildings are fantastic and both take up an unused part of the land not compromising the house at all. You would never have thought it was possible, but it was. It has been a fantastic outcome both in the kind of tenant it has attracted as well as the healthy rental return I receive.

Again, think ahead about what sort of support you have and what kind of help you will need in future years. Will you move into the Granny Flat eventually and could your children, for example, move into the family home - or will you ensure a Property Manager selects a premium family tenant for your family home?

In Summary

As discussed earlier in this chapter, there are pros and cons to any decision you will make. If you have a life partner, you will need to consider what you both want and each other's needs; your decision should not be hasty. I highly recommend you thoroughly investigate every option and go with the one you feel most comfortable with and gives you the best 'gut feeling'.

You may find it interesting to note that your 'gut feeling' is a combination of your experience and innate knowing. I am sure you would have had an enormous amount of experience in your life and your innate knowing, if you are not in a state of stress, should be your best guide. Going with your gut, rather than on someone else's opinion is imperative. Trust what it is telling you.

Rightsizing Made Easy – Getting Ready For Take-Off!

Please Don't Throw My Memories Away!

Many Empty Nesters believe that moving into a new home means they must throw most of their treasured items away. This is one of the biggest inhibitors moving forward. It can immobilise people and make them shudder with fear. This thought can make them bury their head deep in the sand. *Does this sound like you?*

I'm here to tell you that it's not the case. I like to look at de-cluttering as an opportunity to cleanse the clutter at home as well as the soul, an experience to be enjoyed where you have the chance to get your life and belongings simplified and in order. My clients tell me how fabulous they feel afterwards! It not only makes you feel fabulous but also leaves you with a deep sense of long-lasting achievement. A long-term weight that you have been carrying around for years will be lifted from your shoulders.

I often hear clients say things like:

"But don't throw my memories away."
"I have been meaning to do this for so long."
"I know it has to be done, but I just don't know where to begin."
"How can I start if I don't know where I'm going to move to?"
"My children tell me when I'm gone, they will be hiring a skip."

It's not a matter of throwing everything away that won't fit into your new home. It is purely a matter of allocating time and working through your things in a rational and organised manner.

It is for this reason that we created our 'Rightsize Your Home Framework', a strict plan we use to help our clients move through the process effectively and efficiently. I will share it with you in the following pages, so you can follow it and apply it when it comes time to make your move.

The Framework is a staged and timed process that progressively works through sorting your items at a methodical, sensitive and steady pace, and ensures I do the following with my downsizing coaching clients

The framework involves / incorporates:

- Treasuring memories while decluttering

- Supporting the Empty Nester

- A navigation tool by my team and clients

- A vital part of having a successful move

I'll share the framework with you as well as some further insights into its use along the way. The framework also incorporates the practical experience of the move's logistics as well as integrating Kotter's change management principles.

In regards to sorting through your possessions, wouldn't you prefer to take control and do this yourself rather than have others doing it for you? I couldn't think of anything worse than my children (or anyone else for that matter) deciding what goes where and what personal belongings are to be discarded or thrown away. Only you can truly value your possessions and understand why you choose to keep them; no-one else should be making this decision for you. It's yours to make and yours only. I want you to take control now and allocate the necessary time and commitment to your project.

The Real Meaning Of Value

I am in the business of helping you Rightsize your home which means Rightsizing your personal belongings in the process. I'm talking about you creating your new home with your most loved and valued items and making it super special. Not necessarily the most valuable things in monetary terms, but those that you cherish the most. The items you choose to take may be for sentimental reasons and for the lasting memories they give you. It could be a side table your dear grandfather made or a canvas your four-year-old grandson painted at kindy for you.

These are the belongings that may not necessarily have any monetary value at all, but they still mean the world to you. The more superfluous items could be given away, or donated to others who would value them or find them more useful than you do now.

My 'Rightsize Your Home Framework' applies to personal items as does the decision process for downsizing your property. You need to ask yourself if each piece you pick up currently suits your needs. *Do they still satisfy the purpose you originally purchased them for?*

Ask yourself the following questions to determine the 'real' meaning of value when it comes to your personal belongings:

Rightsize Your Home Value Questions:

- *How much do I love you (the item, not you!)?*
- *Do I love you so much I really have to keep you?*
- *Will I need you when I move from this home?*

- *Do I need you for the property presentation when my home goes on the market?*

- *Am I happy to pay to wrap and box you, pay for someone to lift you, transport you, store you, then transport you to my next home?*

- *Will I still be happy that I have done all that when I go to unwrap you at my new home?*

- *Are you one of my most loved items and are you worthy of a place in my stylish new home?*

- *Do you mean so much to me that I would take you on a year's travel break around Australia?*

I highly recommend you take photos of any items you feel you are going to miss. We work with a photographer who creates beautiful memory books of family homes. The photographer takes pictures of rooms and items and puts them thoughtfully into a treasured book. One client recently purchased four copies of her memory book to give to her children as a keepsake. Something like this will assist you enormously in dealing with the emotions involved in letting go of the things you can't take with you.

The 'Rightsize Your Home Framework'

The following framework is critical to each project we undertake and is suggested for any successful outcome when downsizing for that matter. It will encourage efficiency of time, and there is nil deviation.

If our business didn't follow this framework with each Rightsize, we certainly wouldn't enjoy the high level of client satisfaction and referrals that we do. Also, our clients wouldn't have the peace of mind of knowing where we are up to when asked or feel in control throughout the process. It is a tried and proven strategy we continue to use and improve on, project after project.

Following are the steps of our 'Rightsize Your Home Framework'. At the start of the process is, of course, 'The Decision' which we have already covered. Now, we will elaborate on how we action the logistical tasks. You will find a pictorial representation of the framework, along with a summary of what is involved with further explanations.

Rightsize Your Home Framework – Overview

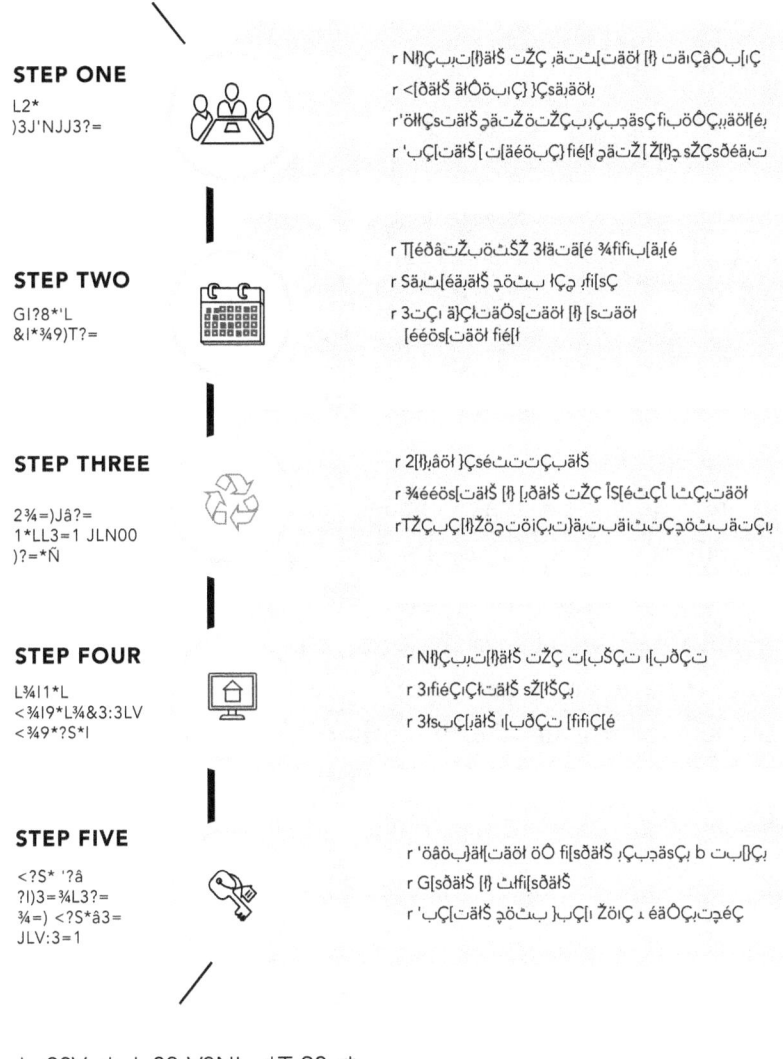

Rightsizing Made Easy - Getting Ready for Take-Off!

The Framework Breakdown – Step-By-Step

This is the initial process of each and every project we work on. This first step is to completely assess the entire project.

Step 1 - The Discussion:

- The discussion of timeframes available
- Sort through what you want to keep
- Assess what items to sell/donate
- Connect with other professionals [financial/legal]

In this step, we go through a 'change readiness review' and a 'needs analysis' for our clients. The questions guide us on how much time we have, how our clients feel about the items in the home, and what sort of idea the client has on when they will be ready to move and where they would like to go. We will also connect them with other professionals, if needed, such as financial advisors, and incorporate them into the Rightsize scope of works.

The questions to be answered here include:

1. Are you the owner of the property?

2. How long have you been living in the home for?

3. Does the home suit your lifestyle any more?

4. Have you decided where you would like to move to?

5. When would you like to have this achieved by?

6. Have you decided whether you are selling or renting your home?

7. What challenges and maintenance requirements do you have at your home?

8. What are the goals you think we can help you achieve?

9. Have you considered the budget you can put towards preparing the property, the move out and the move in?

10. Are you ready for some change and the project ahead?

11. Have you considered all the help and options available to you?

12. What type of help are you looking for?

MOVING CHECKLIST
- found at the back of the book

We have many unique tools we use in our business to help our clients managing the downsizing process with ease, including the 'Moving Checklist' you will find located at the back of the book.

This handy checklist is packed with items to use as your compass and markers which will help with pre-planning the move in the early stages. You will need to start some of the checklist items early on, such as some packing and clearing areas to finishing some checklist items once you have arrived in your new home.

Step 2 - Project Breakdown

It's never a major concern whether our clients know exactly where they are going to move to, or not. The exercise of decluttering is often about taking back control, Rightsizing what is in the house, presenting 'ready for market' and then considering the 'where to' can be done later. Either way is fine.

With decluttering and presentation taken care of, our clients feel freer to look around at housing choices and options. This Initial Appraisal is a stress-relief and a game changer for readiness. In most cases, when the client has already found a new home, they tend to be more motivated throughout the process to get the job done.

When we commence the Initial Appraisal, we go through the initial discussion questions and responses on a far deeper level. We will define the dates (albeit approximately) and work out in detail what kind of help the owners are looking for. We will also take a thorough online walk-through of the property and complete a suggested Project Plan Schedule..

Our owners always have two options: they can either use all of our advice given at the Initial Appraisal and we can provide a complete stress-free solution, or they can choose to engage their own trades and services and manage the project themselves.

By completing this Initial Appraisal with our team, our clients end up with a defined and complete list of things to do so they can proceed with confidence and work toward their final goal. In case you were wondering, we do charge a small fee for our Initial Appraisal service and our clients always find it very valuable and well worth the outlay.

You can find out more at www.propertymakeoveracademy.com.au

Online Walk-Through - Maintenance And Presentation Focus

In the Initial Appraisal online walk-through, we complete two activities concurrently. We look at what needs to be done on a maintenance level and then we discuss how to best present your property for sale.

Knowing the 'ins and outs' of your buyer target market is imperative to present your home in the right manner and increase the appeal. There are a number of target market options, so you will need to investigate who your target market is with an expert. For now, I will focus on the maintenance and presentation basics.

I always complete the walk-through as though I am seeing your home in the same way a potential buyer will see it, for the first time. I make sure I walk-through in the same way a potential purchaser would in order to give you a jump start, so you know what they will look for and comment on. Our Initial Appraisal documentation is written in this format.

So, if you were a purchaser, what would you be looking for?

As a minimum you would want to see that;
- The property is well-maintained and appears to be low-maintenance

- The property must be clean and ready for occupancy
- The property's best selling points need to be presented in the way your market wants to see them (polish the diamond).
- There are opportunities for enhancements, especially in line with what the target market is looking for.

This property walk-through process requires a list of all the room names to be collated as you go. Always start on the street, at the front of the property and switch your thinking hat. You are now wearing the hat of the property's potential purchaser. Get your clipboard, your coloured dot stickers and pen - here we go!

Find your Online Walk-Through Checklists Following.

Online Walk Through Checklist: Areas of Opportunity

Area	Action to be taken	Allocation to/date
Street Appeal		
Medium Strip		
Front fence		
Garden		
Driveway		
Entry way		
Front porch/deck		
Windows		
Window coverings		
Entry Area		

Online Walk Through Checklist: *Areas of Opportunity*

Area	Action to be taken	Allocation to/date
Living Room		
Casual Dining		
Dining Room		
Kitchen		
Hallway		
Rear Porch/Deck		
Stairs		
Bedroom 1		
Bedroom 2		
Bedroom 3		

Copyright © 2020. Rightsize Your Home. All rights reserved.

Online Walk Through Checklist: Areas of Opportunity

Area	Action to be taken	Allocation to/date
Study / Bedroom 4		
Bathroom 1		
Bathroom 2		
Bathroom 3		
Under stairs / storage		
Garage/s and carports		
Shed		
Other		

Copyright © 2020. Rightsize Your Home. All rights reserved.

Online Walk-Through - New Home Floor Plan Review & Placements

Now is the time to acknowledge that your current home and your new 'Rightsize' Home will look quite different. All of the items that occupy your space now will not be able to come with you.

On the following page, I have given an example of a two bedroom flat or villa. This is the format of floor plan that you will need to either:

1. Redraw from memory of the new place you have purchased, or;
2. Visualise the more appropriate sized place you would like to find.

Once you have a similar layout in your mind or on paper, you can complete your property walk through to help generate the action items you need to address.

If you can visualise your new floor plan, this will help you understand exactly how much you can bring with you and you will be able to sort through your things methodically.

If you already have an idea of where you are going or found your new place of residence, you can draw that. If not, you can just invent one if it is a 'desired option' at this stage. Make sure you refer to your 'wish list' at the beginning of the book. *How many rooms will you need, would you like an outdoor entertaining area? etc.*

Take note of the floor area and the space allocation to bedrooms and/or study etc. If you have this drawing handy when you complete your walk-through, you may begin to see what items can come with you and what will have to go. You will need to code the rooms on the floor plan to match your current furniture. This is where you will use your coloured dot stickers.

Visualise your new living space. This is an example of a blank floor plan so you can visualise your new living space.

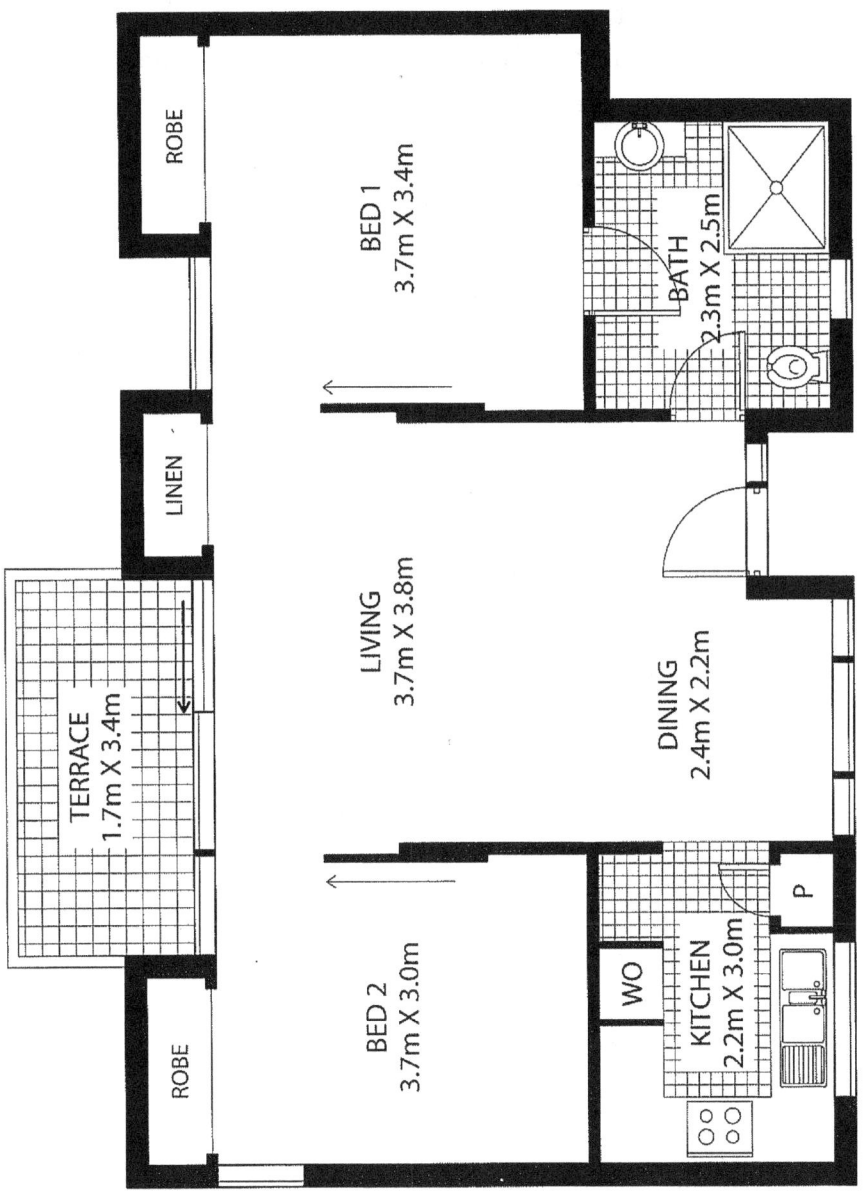

Next, you will need to develop this floor plan (or potential one), by cutting out a series of scaled 'Keep' items of furniture. Now, match the items you want to take against the location on the floor plan where the inventory is to go. It is necessary to work out the holding ability of the rooms with the furniture pieces compared to your plan.

You will also need to work out the holding ability of the storage areas against the items that you currently have held in cupboards, drawers and even hanging on the wall. You will need to flag what can go with you and what should not.

You will love the new technology available which will enable your downsizing of cables, CD's and computers! This means things like having the internet on the TV, making Skype calls with the grandchildren a whole lot more convenient. Wireless technology, means limiting the cable jungle. You can even consider embracing change of music technology with music systems like Sonos or Spotify and eliminating all of the CD's, as well as changing to mobile devices.

This will allow you to determine whether you need to organise more joinery for when you arrive in your new home (if the space will allow it)! Oh no! *Could it be time to cull that shoe and hat collection?*

Of course, some of your furniture items will go to your new home but will not be able to stay for the market presentation. You will need to mark these items in a different colour as they will need to go into temporary storage during the sales and marketing campaign, before moving to your new home.

This is the time to 'let go' of any items that cannot come with you. Paying to store items permanently is going to cost you money and is not recommended.

Make Notes. *Mark the items you would like to keep on your new floor plan.*

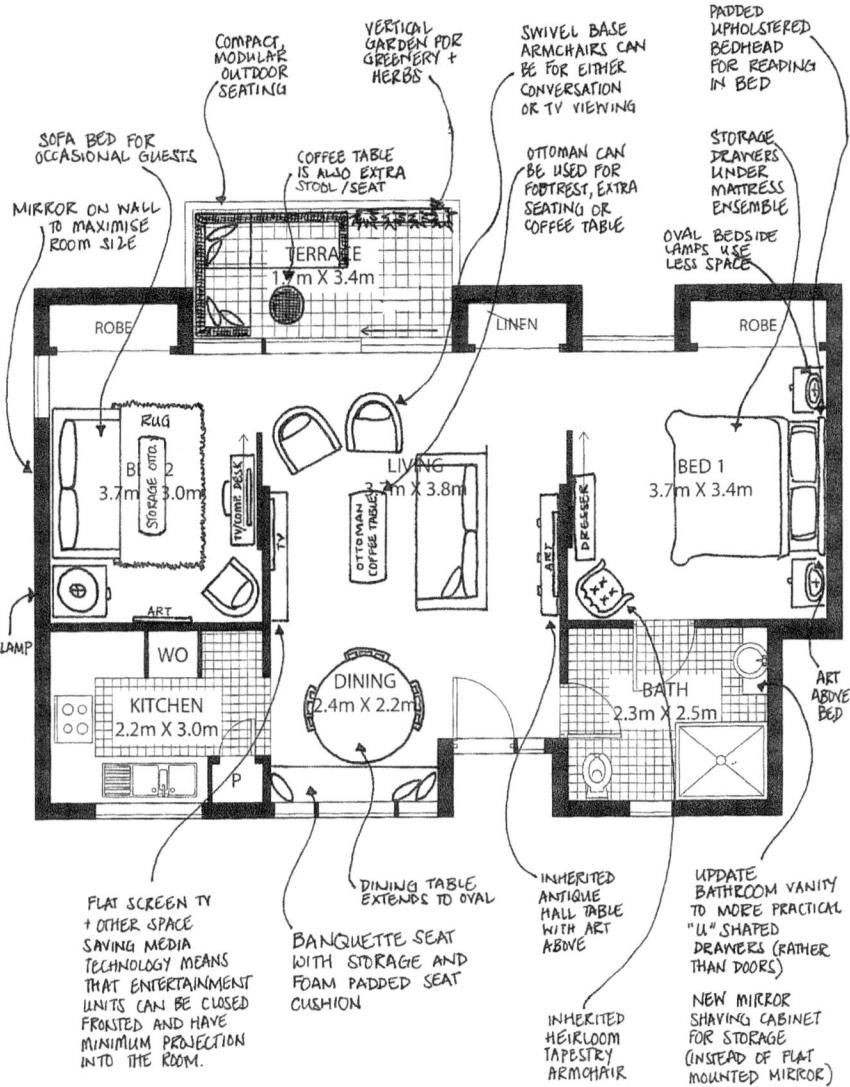

Rightsizing Made Easy - Getting Ready for Take-Off!

Time Management For Room Packing

At this stage, it's important to discuss the excess items of furniture and contents. Again, you will need to use the coloured 'dot' labelling system. These items need to be worked through to identify which ones to sell, donate or 'toss'. You will need to read on for an understanding of how to make these decisions and where the items are best to go.

We have added an example inventory list template with example colours at the top and a template for your use:

Example: Unwanted Items Disbursement List:
(cut down version)

Location	Item	Disbursement
Garden	Bird Bath	eBay (Green dot)
	Excess Potted Plants	Brother (Red dot)
Entry way	Umbrella Stand	Charity (Blue dot)
Front porch/deck	Outdoor Setting	Charity (Blue dot)
	Potted Plant	Uncle (Yellow dot)

Your Unwanted Items Disbursement List:

Location	Item	Disbursement
Internal Areas		
Entry Area		
Living Room		
Casual Dining		
Dining Room		
Kitchen		
Hallway		
Rear Porch/Deck		
Stairs		
Bedroom 1		

Your Unwanted Items Disbursement List:

Location	Item	Disbursement
Bedroom 2		
Bedroom 3		
Bedroom 4		
Study/Bedroom 5		
Bathroom 1		
Bathroom 2		
Bathroom 3		
Under Stairs/Storage		
Garage/s and Carports		
Shed		
Other		

I am sure that after completing the unwanted items disbursement checklist, you will be feeling much better or maybe a little torn between which items to leave and which to bring with you. You may even notice a feeling of sadness at this stage but it is good to remember this as a natural part of change.

The next checklist to fill out is about allocating your processing or 'doing' time. You will need to allocate time to moving or processing the inventory list for sale, for donation and for rubbish.

The contents of the furniture need the same processing, so you will need to have allocated time to call up the various recipients of donations, or the waste/recycling service providers to discuss and organise, manage and finally to make it happen.

The same format of the list can be used to allocate the amount of time required to your project by each area of the home. You can then transfer this information to your diary and call up your willing helpers to book them in!

You will begin to feel you are undertaking a job at this stage, and you are in the managerial position. As with any role, it is essential to plan out each step, and all of the Checklists have been designed to help you do just that.

So, let's continue. You are now one step closer and doing a fantastic job!!

Decluttering and Presentation Hours Allocation

Area	Decluttering Hours	Responsibility / Who	Presentation Hours	Responsibility / Who
Street Appeal				
Medium Strip				
Front Fence				
Garden				
Driveway				
Entry Way				
Front Porch/ Deck				
Windows				
Window Coverings				
Internal Areas				
Entry Area				

Copyright © 2020. Rightsize Your Home. All rights reserved.

Decluttering and Presentation Hours Allocation

Area	Decluttering Hours	Responsibility / Who	Presentation Hours	Responsibility / Who
Living Room				
Casual Dining				
Dining Room				
Kitchen				
Hallway				
Rear Porch/ Deck				
Stairs				
Bedroom 1				
Bedroom 2				
Bedroom 3				
Bedroom 4				

Copyright © 2020. Rightsize Your Home. All rights reserved.

Decluttering and Presentation Hours Allocation

Area	Decluttering Hours	Responsibility / Who	Presentation Hours	Responsibility / Who
Study / Bedroom 5				
Bathroom 1				
Bathroom 2				
Bathroom 3				
Under Stairs / Storage				
Garage/s and Carports				
Shed				
Other				

Copyright © 2020. Rightsize Your Home. All rights reserved.

By the end of this Initial Appraisal, you will have:

1. Completed a thorough walk-through of your property and noted all items of change required.

2. Noted all pieces of furniture that can be taken to your new place, and all others to go for sale or to family/friends, donation or charity.

3. Estimated the amount of hours by room for the decluttering, packing and presentation, and booked help on your calendar.

4. Requested a removalist and storage quote to your new home

By the end of the Initial Appraisal your inventory notes will have furniture lists for:

1. Items for the new home – stay for presentation

2. Items for the new home – store for presentation

3. Items not for the new home – eBay, auction house, Facebook Marketplace or Gumtree, donations to friends or family, charity pick-up or waste/recycling.

Step 3 – Hands-On - Getting stuff done!

This step is about the 'doing'. Your aim here should be to de-clutter and neutralise your space and only leave behind the basics you need for living so you can present your home for market. The rest should be boxed up and stored temporarily, to be delivered to your new home when you are ready.

Now is the time to print or draw the floor plan of your new home, stick it up on the wall and write up the room code names and the schedule. Nominate a date for pack-up completion.

A copy of this floor plan with room codes should be copied for your removalist so they know precisely where your coded boxes will go. You can also choose to use coloured dots.

Code examples are:

Kitchen: K
Living Room: LR
Master Bedrooms: BM
Ensuite: ES
Guest Bedroom: BG
2nd Bedroom: B2
Garage: G

You will be making room-by-room decisions on items and breaking down the process of organising, so it does not get too overwhelming. You will need to decide what to keep, sell, donate or 'toss.'

As we discussed earlier, it's important to revisit the real meaning of 'value' here. *Do you love each item you are choosing to keep? Do you need it anymore?*

And lastly, what will you do with the items you've decided to keep, sell, donate or 'toss'? Which service providers can help you in regards to rubbish removal, auctioneers, trades and other services?

Let's do it! Create allocated areas in your home to assemble the listed inventory items. This is the time to start your estimated hours for implementation. I always suggest starting with your garage, spare bedrooms and other storage areas as they will give you a quick win. They also may double as your 'transit items', rooms of allocated spaces for your items on their way out.

You will need the following items to take into your scheduled rooms as you work through:

- Rubbish bags (two different colours indicating a colour each for donations and garbage) as well as your council rubbish bin.
- Cardboard boxes for recycling as well as the council recycling bins.
- A box for items in the wrong room that belong in a different place.
- Cleaning equipment and personal protection.

- Boxes to pack items for transport with paper, pens, and markers for inventory lists and coding/ labelling boxes.

Go through every drawer in every room, ask yourself the value questions and move items to the allocated areas.

How To Keep Things You Need

The value questions apply to this particular decision as well as a logistical check to see if an item can physically fit. One of the most compelling stories I have heard is one that my eBay trader shared.

He talks about a client who moved homes and thought it best that he hire a large storage shed to keep items he believed were quite treasured.

He ended up hiring long-term storage to keep these items and thought better of it a few years later. He asked my trader to come down and look at his shed and then action the inventory for sale. The eBay trader ended up selling his more valuable items for $4,000 although he had spent $11,000 in storage costs (not to mention the emotional worry of thinking about that shed all the time). It would have been much more sensible if he answered the value questions correctly and if the eBay or auctioneering process had taken place at the time he was transitioning.

I have also had clients who were storing their daughter's furniture while she was living overseas. As it turns out the family home is of 'heritage' style and the furniture was too contemporary for the styling process, so it will have to be moved out. In the meantime, the furniture has also become out-dated. Their daughter's furniture, stored in the home for ten years is no longer needed.

So what do the parents do? Pay for storage or should they sell it? Another tricky situation.

Selecting the items coming with you should be a pleasurable process. Just think, you will have less to worry about, less to clean, less to organise and a chance to reflect when thinking about these decisions.

The lovely part is that your next chapter is open and your new home will only play host to your treasured personal items. Many of our clients revel in sorting and decluttering. They love having the freedom to 'cull' items they didn't love that much and can use the opportunity to save on transport costs and buy something special for their new place. They often wish they had done it earlier.

The 'Rightsize Your Home' value questions apply here as discussed earlier. If you can remember to question yourself with these fairly and honestly, the process will work.

How To Sell Things You Don't Need

Once you've decided on the items that aren't coming with you and you have chosen not to gift them, they are for sale!

There are many places these items can go, the key ones of which I've listed below:

Garage Sale

You may opt for this because of the benefits it can bring and the ease with which it can be carried out. One reason is practicality – the buyers come to you. Second, it can help the environment with most goods going into homes and not to landfill. Some examples of supporting websites are eGarage Sale and Garage Sale Trail.

The potential negative side of this is the privacy issue. Personally, I do worry about my clients holding these sales as they do involve sacrificing a lot of time, energy and privacy. It may also be a sign for neighbours to gossip.

You can choose to worry about this or not. You may find some of your neighbours would like to offer a hand and help you throughout the process. They may even come and keep you company on the day.

If they have some clearing out to do, you may like to ask them if they would like to bring some items up to sell as well. The idea here is to try and keep your spirits up and enjoy the process. More hands always make light work. Ask your Grandchildren to help - you might like to hire them and pay them for manning the stall for you.

You will find some people may come very early to your garage sale. These people are on the hunt for valuable items they can upsell and do this kind of thing for a living.

Any items that are authentically retro and in excellent condition will sell for a decent price. The younger generation love these items and will pay for them. Don't give them away!!

Here are some things to consider if you choose to have a garage sale:

- Moving the items to the garage
- Advertising
- Questions all day

- Manning the garage all day with back-ups for break times
- The early starters coming at 6 am
- Unpredictable weather

If you are up for it, then it may be just perfect for you. There are some free checklists to help you have a successful sale so head to the internet and gather the information. Forewarned is forearmed.

So how do you plan a garage sale? I researched and found these useful tips to help you get organised.

Plan your garage sale 30 days in advance. Avoid public holidays or long weekends if you are not living in a town or area that attracts crowds at these times. Choose weekends for obvious reasons. Make sure there are no local community events that will be on the same day. Check with your local council for by-laws covering this type of event.

Invite your neighbours! They might want to partake in this event creating a street event and cost share. Create flyers to distribute to each home in your neighbourhood.

Advertising is the most critical stage of having a successful sale. Ask your local real estate agent if they have any supporting material.

On the morning of the day of the sale, put up some banners, posters, balloons at each end of the street, or anything to attract people to check out your goods. Don't forget to clean up afterward!

Garage Sale Checklist:

- Choose a clear, open space in your front yard to place your goods.
- Make a list of the goods and estimate how much you want to sell each one for. Buyers will be haggling so make a price range for each item.
- You may like to have three trestle tables. One table can be items selling from $1-3, one trestle table may be $3-10, and one trestle table may be $10 plus.
- Make a plan on how you would arrange the items in your yard. Make your items as clean, visible and attractive as possible.
- Have plenty of loose change.
- Some early birds may knock on your door; it is best to be ready bright and early on the day of the sale.
- Keep your house locked during the event.

eBay

Launched in 1995, eBay started as a place to trade collectibles and hard-to-find items. Today, eBay is a global marketplace where you can buy and sell just about anything.

I am looking after a client as I write this, who is doing the whole 'Rightsize' project. We are making over his home so he can enjoy this for a year or two, with the intention of selling in the short to medium term. Here are the items on his Ebay trading list:

- Entire Kitchen

- Appliances
- Flute
- Chair and Footrest
- French Doors
- Antiques
- Light Fittings

If a client wants to sell something, we refer them to an eBay trader who generally uses the guideline of a $50 minimum value per item to be sold. An eBay trader will work on a commission percentage, so it is in their best interest to help you achieve a high price.

There are many tricks of the trade, and if you are not a regular eBayer, I suggest you read up on the process and the hints provided to be successful. If you do not fancy taking on another full-time job while trying to manage the rest of the downsizing process, I do not blame you! The actual process of selling on eBay is quite involved. If someone you know is handling this side of things as a favour to you, consider paying them for their time, as it may become quite arduous. I would advise engaging an independent eBay trader as a preference.

Trading assistants love their work. They find it exciting and challenging to get the most for you. Review their track record and make sure they are a great seller and have excellent feedback. After all, you are trusting them with your valuable items and you want to make sure you get a good return.

Your trader will come to your property and check off the inventory. You will need to sign off on each agreed item, the reserve price, if you request one, and the time period for each sale to occur. The trader will photograph it, measure it, take note of all the details like maker's marks and form etc and then list it online. You will need to provide them with the best possible history you can. If you have some original sale dockets etc, and the original packaging, this will help enormously.

Auction Houses

Antiques and other highly sought after items can sell well at Auction Houses. An Auctioneer can help you find the value of each piece by looking up the history of similar items sold. They will send a representative to your home and will arrange a time to pick up the agreed items for sale. Auction Houses have monthly sales and will promote your items of value on their website and through their database, leading up to the auction. Some Auction Houses deal with higher-end items than others. It is best to choose the most suitable according to your needs.

Gumtree

Gumtree launched in Australia back in 2007 as a local classified ads and a community site. It was designed to connect people who were either planning to move or had just arrived in a new neighbourhood and needed help getting started with accommodation, employment and meeting new people.

The Gumtree website is global now and is for local community classifieds including stuff for sale, cars, flat share, flat rentals and jobs - essentially working in a similar manner to eBay.

Facebook

There are many community hubs on Facebook and local Buy, Sell and Swap Groups. If you know your way around Facebook, this method of selling can be useful and efficient. The only issue you may have is people claiming that they will pay on pick-up and never arrive. It can be a little frustrating, however, it's unavoidable and should not deter you.

How To Donate Things You Don't Need

Gifting unwanted items to charity would have to be my favourite part of the disbursement process. Your unwanted items can be sold with the proceeds helping people in need or they can be passed on directly to those in need.

We can refer many organisations you can choose to donate to and selecting one that helps a cause close to your heart makes it even easier to 'let go' of things you may not need anymore.

For example, in our local area we have a women's shelter that looks after women at risk and helps them get back on their feet. We also have local book fairs and, of course, outlets like Salvation Army, St.Vincent de Paul and Lifeline. Many of my clients feel better when they know where their goods will be going and who they will be helping.

'Give Now' is a practical place to explore all the different ways you can help the community. Find out how to make a donation, how to get involved, how and where to join in and support your community. If you visit the site, you will find great ways to help communities, both large and small.

'Freecycle' is a grassroots non-for-profit movement of people who are giving (and getting) stuff for free in their towns. It's all about reuse and reducing landfill. In fact, it's the most extensive recycling and reuse website in the world!

From a logistical sense while you are organising your Rightsizing, always keep a box near the front door that you can drop items into every day. If you have a charity pick-up service, then have a regular booking with them so that your unwanted items head out the door instead of back into the house!

If you have no pick-up service, then you could put a box into the car every now and again. If you keep the momentum going, you will gradually get on top of things!

How To Toss Things You Don't Need

As discussed, it is best to ask yourself if you can donate, sell, give-away or recycle before you just throw something away. A big part of my job is to ensure we minimise the amount that goes to landfill.

Keeping boxes near the door goes for your rubbish as well. Take the time as you are decluttering to ensure your rubbish is separated for the bins and use your recycling bins accordingly. Most Councils have a hard rubbish day once a year. However, through some Councils you can order one or two additional pick-ups from your nature-strip for a minimal cost per year. They do have clear guidelines about what you can put out and what you cannot.

Example Items Accepted:

Mattresses and bed bases, scrap metal, non-recyclable household items, televisions, stereo equipment, appliances, timber in pieces no longer than 1.5 metres, carpet, metal tools and equipment, hot water systems, lawn mowers, whitegoods including fridges (remove door), washing machines, air conditioners and stoves.

Example Items Not Accepted:

Car tyres, batteries, garden waste, recyclables, household waste, glass (sheet glss, mirrors, windows, glass tables), building or renovation materials, gas cylinders, chemicals, oils, pesticides, paint, asbestos, hazardous waste, bricks, concrete, rubble, soil, cement sheeting and engine blocks.

If you have a hard waste rubbish removal coming up, make the most of it, even if your move is not imminent.

Step 4 – Target Marketability Makeover

As discussed earlier, preparing your home for the right target market is essential and will help you appeal to more than just the local developer looking for a bargain.

Understanding the target market with the help of your local agent or property makeover specialist at 'walk-through' stage will help you understand the need for potential changes to your home. Don't worry if you cannot visualise the changes; you will need to trust the professionals you are working with because if they are suggesting improvements and modifications, they will have your best interests at heart.

For both sale and rentals, there are certain things your ideal target market will want to see which you will need to address. You can read more about this in the next chapter - Attracting The Flocks - where I share my *7 Secret Tips To Property Selling Power*.

Meeting this expectation will draw more people into the interested pool of potential purchasers, which will, in turn, facilitate a more efficient and profitable sale. Correct preparation will also ensure that your market will not be 'scared off' or think your property is a 'project' and too expensive to 'manage.'

There are a few properties this does not apply to (the 1%) which are either:

1. Facing an imminent and immediate bulldozer - due to development and the fact that the properties adjacent are all awaiting the same fate! Or,

2. The property is unsafe and uninhabitable.

Even in this case, we suggest that you present your home adequately. If the developer can quickly rent out your property while they submit plans to the Council, this will mean they can subsidise their mortgage while waiting for their plans to be approved. In some cases this can take years. Therefore, even in this case, the property must be presentable in appearance for a tenant to move straight in.

Many downsizers are resigned to the fact that their property will be bull-dozed and do not believe spending money will help them. This mindset can see many people miss out on really potentialising their property.

It is more than likely that every property owner reading this will have a property that they should present well for the market. It is critical to broadening your market appeal, and I urge you to have a good read of the following chapter to help you identify and make changes to your property that will help you attract as many people as possible.

Step 5 – Move Coordination And Move-In Makeover

The final item on the 'Rightsize Your Home Framework' is the transport day. Your place is sold or rented out, and it's time to go. If you are moving next door to your new flat, or Granny Flat, then the project is still the same – you just won't have as far to travel. In fact, you may not even require the truck, just the removalist team.

According to the floor plan formulated at the Initial Appraisal stage, everyone will be aware of what furniture is to go where in your new home and you can transition smoothly. You can use the Moving Checklist to navigate your way through items and when relocating. We use this with our clients and find this system is the best way to have a stress-free move day!

Once again, this Checklist involves your new home floor plan as mentioned previously. By giving every room a colour or a code and making sure all your boxes are marked on the top and side with the same code, you can have each box placed in the correct room for unpacking.

When you get to the property, place the correct highly visible colour or number on the door of the corresponding room. If you follow this system, your removalists will take the boxes and furniture immediately to the right area. This exercise is crucial because there will not be additional lifting required once the removalists have gone.

The Pre-Sale Nest Makeover – Attracting The Flocks

My 7 Secrets to Property Selling Power

How real estate has changed over the years. We have touched on this subject in our previous chapters, but here I will elaborate more. Your typical buyer's expectations have changed significantly from when you last sold as well as the industry that manages the sales (and rentals). So much so that I have developed a very successful downsizing business at belindawoolrych.com, as well as the Property Makeover Acedemy for those that want to complete their own projects with direction from my coaching and programs.

The business is continuously booked with pre-sale property appraisals and project coordination, day in and day out. In these appraisals, we have a particular way of evaluating the target market requirements - interpreting and applying these changes to every property that we have been engaged to manage that is going on the market.

We aim to ensure that each property we makeover meets the expectations of potential purchasers. We want the 'offer' and the 'needs and wants' to connect. Our business is in high demand because the buyers' expectations are increasing and sellers need to keep up with the competition. If they choose not to prepare their home for sale adequately, they cannot expect to achieve the same result.

If your property presents well, then you are increasing your pool of potential purchasers. Investors will have an opportunity to build and have someone move in straight away, to ensure an immediate rental return. If the property is not well presented, investors may not be able to see the potential or will consider the presentation work required too costly from a Return-On-Investment (ROI), time and money perspective.

Now I wish to share my *7 Secrets To Property Selling Power* that forms the basis of our on-site property appraisals. I believe they encompass the entire nature of our business. You will find some great tips to help you move through the sales or leasing process successfully.

Essentially, the property sale and rental marketing follow the same approach as far as presentation goes and, if you read-on, you will understand why. Our Property Makeover Specialists have proved this philosophy time and again. They follow these secrets with every visit and tailor them personally to each client when on site.

Pre-sale presentation or pre-sale styling is a 'no-brainer'! If you don't present your property to your target market in the most positive light, you may be alienating areas of your potential market. The job of the Property Makeover Specialist is to create the largest pool of potential buyers possible, therefore positioning you to achieve the best possible outcome for the efficiency of sale and profitability.

I have heard stories of homes going on to the market unprepared and sitting on the market for months. It is best not to feel rushed into selling at this stage by a real estate agent or anyone else and miss your chance to achieve an excellent return on your investment.

When listing your property for sale, you want the entire process to be as stress-free and financially rewarding as possible. Have you thought to yourself, *"What can I do to make the most out of this property sale?"* Did you know you have just 15 seconds to create a lasting positive first impression with your property? You don't get a second chance at a first impression – so make it work the FIRST time!

My pre-sale business focuses the following key questions on the mind of every client. You may have also asked yourself these questions.

- **How can I get my property looking its best without spending more than I need to, so I don't overcapitalise and waste my money?**

Understandably, there is an immediate concern for investing money into a property that you are about to sell. *Will we get our money back? Will we be wasting money?* Overcapitalising is a taboo word in our business - we go to extreme measures to ensure you achieve a substantial return on your investment.

- **How can I identify what potential clients will be looking for, so I can minimise the faults and highlight the good points, without being dishonest?**

A mistake you may make is usually because you have not thought about who the property will appeal to and therefore not have an understanding of what the buyers will be looking for.

Clients typically think about the features of the property they like, as if they were looking to stay in the property or re-purchase it. They don't think about what features will attract a different person: the potential purchaser.

Every change you make when preparing your property for sale is about appealing to your target market, and it is critical that you know the identity of these people. *Who are they? Where are they from? How do they live? What do they do? What do they want from the property? What will increase competition for the sale?*

My process is know for getting it right when presenting and successfully attracting the flocks.

- ***What are the secrets to having a steady flow of traffic at an open house?***

If your home presents in the best manner and your agent organises a professional photographer and implements a good campaign, you have every chance of achieving your dream sale price. In some cases, we exceed our client's expectations. It is not unusual to gain $50, $100 or even $200k over the original property valuation. This kind of result is not unheard of, especially if you make someone fall in love with your home and they buy from an emotional perspective. This is ultimately your perfect buyer, and your goal is to draw them in.

- ***What should I avoid doing?***

Avoid doing absolutely nothing to present your home for sale - unless you are prepared to accept that your property may sit on the market and become 'stale', or may not achieve the potential price it deserves. You should avoid listening to unqualified advice, avoid listening to Real Estate Agents who want to rush you and believe in volume-selling and, most importantly, avoid listening to people who don't know what they are talking about!

- ***Is it worth removing, hiring or rearranging furniture? How do I decide what's needed to have every room looking great?***

Yes, it is usually worth swapping some furniture around, making sure the space is allocated to the target market needs. In most cases, homes do need some updates in furnishings and are well advised to declutter and 'present' well. This may involve hiring some furniture. You can decide on these items by asking for professional presentation advice from a pre-sale specialist company, like belindawoolrych.com

So here are **My 7 Secrets To Property Selling Power.** I have developed these from my experience making over properties for a number of years and they underpin every Initial Appraisal site visit. They are the foundation of how we approach our jobs and maximise our clients' investments.

My 7 Secrets To Property Selling Power

Secret #1: Let Go And Think Like A Buyer

Thinking like a buyer is a difficult switch for a vendor to make. I always ask our clients... *"How old were you when you bought the property, and what made you fall in love with it?"*

Letting go and thinking like a buyer is often a challenge for our vendors. It is important to change your thinking process about your property.

Now as an owner, decisions (and changes) must be treated as transactional and business-focused and not emotional. You need to apply the mindset that it's not about you anymore! It is about all those potential buyers and what they want.

Remember: Selling isn't about you anymore.

Interestingly, it is often your exact buyer profile (i.e. the younger you) that will be purchasing the property. So it is our job to ask clients to take their 'owner' hat off and put their 'buyer' hat on.

Remembering what the property was like when you first moved in, we want to know what it was you fell in love with and made you buy the property. This reason may be similar for your potential purchasers.

Hot Tip - Take your 'Owner Hat' off; Put your 'Buyer Hat' on!

Again, it's not about you anymore. It's about the target market and the buyer who is going to write your cheque! It's probable they will like the same features, however you need to understand they are looking for different things than you.

One of my favourite clients talked about this 'Hot Tip' being a major turning point in selling his property. He told me it wasn't until we talked about 'switching hats' that this happened.

"I had been thinking as the owner. I knew what I paid for my property, what other properties in the street were selling for, and was looking at the property knowing how I was living in it. I hadn't given any thought as to how someone new would think about my property. I hadn't thought about showing off its versatility and highlighting what they would be looking for." Stefan, Mona Vale

I know how hard it can be to disconnect from something you know and love. No matter the reason for the sale, you may always have an emotional connection to your property.

Now is the time to help your prospective buyers connect with your property so that you can ensure an effective sale, minimising your time and maximising your money.

Secret #2: Know Your Market

Pay attention to your buyer target market. Your potential buyers hold the key to the value of your property and they may well be the ones paying off your mortgage! You need to afford them an enormous amount of your thinking.

When considering presenting your property for this market, don't think about what you like; think about them and how to appeal to them all. You are really not the main consideration in this transaction, I'm afraid. Your potential purchaser or target market will be visiting your property and imagining themselves living there and making it their home.

Potential purchasers study the market for a long time prior to a purchase, sometimes years. They will know!

Questions to consider...

How will your potential purchaser live?

How does your property suit their family?

How will they get to work and school?

How much time will maintenance take?

How will they place their furniture?

How long will they stay?

Will their children like it?

Is the garden easy to maintain?

The list goes on and on.

Hot Tip – Quiz Your Agent!

Your Real Estate Agent should know exactly what type of person is buying properties in your area.

Quiz them and find out how much experience they have, ask them about what sort of buyers are the most likely to be interested in your property.

Are they singles, are they couples, DINKS (Dual Income No KidS), TINKS (Triple Income No KidS), downsizers, retirees, teenage families, toddler families, professional commuters?

From this sort of information, a property makeover specialist can work their magic – and so can you!

Why does this matter?

Examples include: If you are staging for retirees, you should highlight 'easy access.' If you are staging for commuters, you should highlight the 'home office' option.

Staging can set the enticement for any market; you just have to know what each buyer target market is looking for, disconnect yourself (refer to Secret #1), and go with it!

Secret #3: We're Selling! Now think ROI

Here is where we start the sold process early in our minds. This is when the business approach starts to kick in. Your property sale is a significant business transaction.

Being absolutely prepared for and genuine about your move and your beliefs in a positive 'Rightsized' future is all about the power of positive thinking and it starts now.

If you believe in it, it can and will happen.

When in doubt, always consult a professional.

Being a successful business person means you are very careful with your money, of course. We are extremely protective of our clients' money and where they spend it. The same applies with you.

We only want you to invest where a rational decision-making process can result in a good return-on-investment (ROI) for you. We want you to affirm your 'We're Selling' intention and ensure the money you invest is only spent on what that target market is looking for.

I was so disappointed with one visit I made to a client's property who started their makeover prior to my visit. They were so proud of the green kitchen they had invested more than $20,000 in. Unfortunately, it was a kitchen to their taste and did not satisfy the needs of the contemporary target market. This was not going to increase the pool of interested people and had therefore not been a successful investment.

They thought they were doing the right thing by installing a new kitchen but they weren't thinking in 'ROI' mode or doing it for the broad appeal of the next potential owners.

Decluttering is an important part of the process.

I have met property owners whose sale had floundered on the market. They didn't declutter, they didn't present their property well, and they didn't understand or connect with the target market that suited it. Yet once their thinking changed, we ordered the boxes and started the makeover process. And guess what? It all happened!

Who knows how much floundering had cost them?

Many of these costs are intangible and are never to be measured.

Their property would probably have been seen as 'stale'.

Hot Tip – Be A Tenant In Your Own Home!

Don't put money into changing things because you like them – you are now an investor! In fact, if you make any changes it's probably good that you don't like them!

This one is tough – you need to behave as if you have ROI expectations. Say to yourself, "It's not my home anymore, I'm just investing here and will my MARKET like this?"

Those fabulous and expensive imported tiles you have been hankering after might not be the best option now – save that for your next property!

If you are contemplating changing something, STOP and THINK: *is it for you or for your buyer?*

Make the decision and 'move out' of your property in your mind. Bringing in more clutter when the goal is to keep your property sleek and in tip-top shape is a habit or behaviour.

You don't need to buy anything else for this property – unless it is right for your market and your presentation to them. This is a tip that can help your sanity as well as your pocket!

Secret #4: Street Appeal, Take Care Of It

I love this secret so much! I enjoy sharing it at every property visit. I remember the experience of selling my own home. Many years ago, I used to have a home office and this one was located at the front of the property. Agents tell me all the time this is still the case and ever increasing due to the power of the internet! Once you are on the internet, you are open to the world, literally.

First impressions really do count.

This Street Appeal Secret is about the 'rubber-neckers' - the people taking an extra-long stroll by your place or asking granny, aunt, sister, mum or son to take a long drive and circle the property a few times on their behalf.

They are the ones under instruction, who have been told to drive around and report back on what they think of the property and the surrounding neighbourhood. They are thinking things like, *does it look like a project? Is it loved? Can you see the place from the street? What does it look like?*

Street appeal is also about getting people through the 'just driving past' stage and, instead, making sure they actually stop and make it into the property.

It's a first and last impression as the buyers will do the 'drive by' but also leave the inspection and often sit in their car looking at the street appeal, then driving back, time and time again to get a feel for the street and the area.

Street appeal also needs to be shown off with amazing photography. Be sure to get the photographs right as they are the searchable and elimination criteria items on the Internet. Once you have worked really hard and have great photographs in place and the property has been shortlisted for a visit, the buyers will come!

Hot Tip – Be Ready For The 24-Hour Drive-By!

I'm sure you've heard the term 'street appeal' by now. Although it's one of the most frequently mentioned topics in real estate and property presentation, I feel it's one of the most overlooked topics.

Most often property owners feel they only have a little room for improvement of their street appeal. They rip out a few weeds, add in a few stones and think that's enough. Your street appeal will be a key to getting traffic to your open house, so make sure yours will pull the buyers in.

As I've said before, don't be surprised if your potential buyers and their 'advisers' all want to (or are being told to) drive past your place to check it out before the open house. You've got to really push to make your street appeal stand out.

You need to make sure you are ready to be on show 24 hours a day, as not everyone can fit in your 10am open home slot. You have diary clashes for lots of people, including city workers, commuters and shift workers buying property. Be ready for them! Get the look, the lighting from dusk until late and the landscaping working for you.

Secret #5: WOW Rooms

Think back to the reason you originally fell in love with your property.

What happened?

Were you an investor who saw something of potential?

Was it the family home connection that you felt?

Where were you and what was it that did it for you?

Chances are it's the same for the next buyer. Make sure you know this and make it the centre of your property presentation strategy.

What is a WOW Room? As the name suggests, it's a room that makes the prospective buyer think "WOW" when they take a look inside, or it could even be an outdoor area.

WOW Rooms are a MUST when staging.

WOW ROOMS are an opportunity to 'show off' one or more great features of your home that sing the song a future buyer wants to hear - they are an amazing opportunity to connect the emotion experienced at your property to a potential sale.

It could be the effort that goes into this best WOW feature of your property that joins all of the dots together for the purchaser. WOW Rooms are a must when staging.

Make sure you know what this area is and if you don't know what it is, ask around the agents and even your visitors, friends and family. You need to understand this potential appeal for your target market and really play-up its strengths.

It could be a feature or area that just knocks out the competition in your area.

Hot Tip – Get The Strategy Right With Your Agent!

WOW Rooms trigger an emotional attachment in the prospective buyer's mind. It allows them to see themselves in that particular room much more easily because of the staging.

Decide what the WOW Rooms are and ensure they are one of the first rooms your prospective buyers are taken into by your Agent. It might be the stunning view from your balcony, your amazing living area or your alluring kitchen/dining area. Just make sure you know where your main effort is going and, of course, tailor it to your market (refer: Secret #2) and communicate well with your Real Estate Agent.

WOW Rooms are about showing off, not overdoing it. A trick to a WOW Room is to position furniture to make the room look as large as possible. This doesn't mean leave a huge amount of space, rather keep the room feeling airy and spacious. Also be sure to leave enough walk-through space throughout the property so that buyers don't end up in traffic jams.

Secret #6: Be Market-Ready 7 Days A Week

Don't be surprised if you get a very early call from your Real Estate Agent asking if it's ok to bring a prospective buyer through for a look. You want to sell your property, so you instinctively say "yes", and then what happens?

Your stomach falls to the floor when you realise you never fully cleaned up after last night's dinner!

Utilise our handy 'inspection ready' checklist.

Staying true to the notion that your property must be in showroom condition, seven days a week, will keep you well prepared for anything that comes your way.

In general, interested parties will inspect everything that is attached to the house. So, if you turned your property upside-down, then everything that doesn't fall out (like WIR and kitchen cupboards) will be looked at.

People want to see the storage availability and need to understand if their 'things' will all fit in. All spaces with correctly proportioned furniture and plenty of white space in the cupboards really show off the property to its potential. Every hour you invest in doing this, just as much as the other points, will absolutely reap dividends.

We have a handy 'Inspection-Ready Tips & Tasks Template' for you in the back of this book, we use it with our clients all the time. More templates like these are available from our Makeover Specialists.

Hot Tip – Follow Your Inspection-Ready Tips & Tasks Checklist

You should create a list and check off the things that need to be done, or the things that need to be taken with you as you leave the property.

Follow the list and you will be confident that your property is looking its best! The list should be laminated so you can wipe it clear after every inspection.

You should also have a column for delegating tasks if you have more than one member of the household who can help! Remember, your property will be open to the general public.

The public scrutinises every little detail from top to bottom, inside and out. Prepare and you will be less likely to suffer any negative distractions or feedback and you'll be well on your way to selling your property before you know it!

Inspection-Ready Tips & Tasks - Your Last Minute 'Get Ready' Guide!

Note: Customise and laminate this guide to re-use at every inspection.

	KITCHEN	Responsibility	Date Completed	Notes
	Benches, sink & appliances wiped.			
	Display fresh fruit and flowers.			
	Excess items put away.			
	All dirty dishes into dishwasher or washed up and put away.			
	Kitchen presented as per photography.			

	BATHROOMS	Responsibility	Date Completed	Notes
	Clean sink & benchtop.			
	All toilet seats down & flush toilets.			
	Excess and personal items put away.			
	All bathroom show towels in place.			
	Bathrooms presented as per photography.			

Inspection-Ready Tips & Tasks - Your Last Minute 'Get Ready' Guide!

Note: Customise and laminate this guide to re-use at every inspection.

BEDROOMS	Responsibility	Date Completed	Notes
All beds made and smoothed, cushions & accessories placed as per photography.			
Move all dirty laundry into the washing machine &/or dryer.			
Clothes folded/hung and put away.			
All personal items put away.			
All bedrooms presented as per photography.			

Copyright © 2020. Rightsize Your Home. All rights reserved.

Inspection-Ready Tips & Tasks - Your Last Minute 'Get Ready' Guide!

Note: Customise and laminate this guide to re-use at every inspection.

	LOUNGE ROOM/S & STUDY	Responsibility	Date Completed	Notes
	Place cushions & accessories as per photography.			
	Open blind/window furnishings and doors.			
	Tidy electrical cords, especially TV & computers.			
	Put away personal/private paperwork/items.			
	Area presented as per pre-sale photography.			

	OUTSIDE, STREET APPEAL & OTHER HANDY TIPS	Responsibility	Date Completed	Notes
	Sweep the driveway and porches/decks. Remove any leaves, etc.			
	Open doors where appropriate.			
	Remove personal and excess items.			
	Hide all rubbish bins.			
	Area presented as per pre-sale photography.			

Copyright © 2020. Rightsize Your Home. All rights reserved.

Inspection-Ready Tips & Tasks - Your Last Minute 'Get Ready' Guide!

Note: Customise and laminate this guide to re-use at every inspection.

OUTSIDE, STREET APPEAL & OTHER HANDY TIPS	Responsibility	Date Completed	Notes
Place dog beds, blankets, etc in car.			
Clean up, including any animal food & excrements.			
Display fresh flowers.			
Position all window furnishings to display best view/lighting.			
Turn on all lights/lamps where required.			
Turn all lights on inside & outside. Outside lights need to be turned on at dusk until late.			
Area presented as per pre-sale photography.			

Secret #7: Know Your Competition

Knowing your competition puts you ahead of the race. **Knowledge is power!** This also gives you a complete sense of reality of what the market is wanting and doing and what is on offer. It is critical you know this information so you can talk frankly and realistically with your agent about your property.

Understand what is happening in the current property market.

What are your competitors doing for the dollars they are expecting?

How do those properties stack up against your property?

How long are they taking to sell?

Has anyone taken their property off the market or swapped agents?

Were they asking too much?

Ask your local agent for details around their local sold results with statistics such as days on market, number of groups through and the amount over or under reserve.

With any major asset, as the owner you must know what is going on in the marketplace, what the risks are, what the returns are and what environmental factors are affecting your price. It is as simple as setting up auto alerts in the major real estate websites. Try browsing websites like realestate.com.au and domain.com.au

Hot Tip: Set Auto Alerts And Get Out There Visiting!

How does your property measure up to your competition?

Not sure?

It's time to get on the computer, set your real estate alerts and hop into your car and stay fully up to speed.

Just as your buyers are doing, you need to set your criteria for bedrooms, bathrooms, accessibility, transport, pool/no pool, etc.

You need to put yourself in their shoes (refer to Secret #1) and measure up against your competitors for sale.

You will get to know how well you stack up against your competition and possibly learn a bit about your buyers and what else they can get for their money. Take off the rose coloured glasses though!

Techniques For Pre-Market Presentation

Downsizers' homes often present fairly similar challenges for pre-market presentation. In a typical suburban life-cycle 1960's-70's era home, for example, there are some techniques that I would undertake to gain the maximum interest.

There are normal problems regarding these types of builds in the minds of the potential purchasers. I continuously find the bedrooms are often a little tight, there's no open-plan living and the colours, floor coverings, window furnishings and wallpaper are often dated. These presentation factors can be cosmetic and quick to update, and actioning the changes will improve the presentation enormously. The property will no longer be seen as a 'project' which could potentially drive the price down and repel your ideal purchaser.

In this circumstance, you could put a budget aside ranging from approximately $10,000 to $50,000 plus co-ordination fee. This will depend on the property size and changes recommended. It will also depend on whether or not you need to update some furniture, use them for presentation and then take to their new home. If your home does need a facelift, then it would certainly be my recommendation to spend the money for a successful presentation and an efficient sale.

Typical updates to make the property more appealing would be:

- Window furnishings
- Floor coverings
- Kitchen changes
- Painting
- Landscaping and clearing
- Hiring of furniture

It is vitally important to seek advice from a pre-sale property specialist to ensure you are getting the most cost-effective recipe of changes. Having the project professionally coordinated will help you gather the right feedback, then getting the trades and services organised to make it all happen.

These projects would typically take around 4-6 weeks to organise from start to finish - depending on how organised you are, which will in turn mean the costs will vary. You can outsource most tasks, however, you cannot outsource the decision making decluttering process. You must be there to make sure your items of 'value' come with you and are not lost to any other cause.

From property presentation to final sale (which can usually take 2-6 weeks, the entire process can be completed comfortably in around 3 months - all up!

When planning, we generally work backwards from the desired 'on market' date. This would normally be a Saturday and, prior to that, we work out the date for photography, then the cleaning, etc. In the following pages, I have included our 'Pre-Market Preparation Calendar' for you to use. You will find it very helpful to help organise your timeframe around going on the market.

We use this calendar in our business all the time. When helping clients with their makeover planning and presentation work, we must work backwards from the desired 'on market' date considering school holidays, weather etc. Or, if our clients are unsure of when they can go on the market, we can work through this example list to calculate when the right time would be.

The rules to note are:

1. Book photography 10 days before your first open home.

2. Ensure furniture hire delivery is two days prior to that photography date (ie. 12 days prior to your first open home).

3. Book your cleaner 16 days (then weekly before opens) prior to your first open home.

4. Have four days put aside prior to the cleaner for any floor-sanding required (ie. 20 days prior to your first open home).

5. Have five days prior to the floor-sanding for your painting (ie. 24 days prior to your first open home).

6. For delivery, prior to photography, calculate all the lead times - for example, window and interior furnishings, landscaping, etc.

It is essential to know that the photography date is the critical date. From a pre-market point of view, the first open home is as important and the photography date is the 'do by' date to stick to.

EXAMPLE PRE-MARKET PREPARATION CALENDAR

PROPERTY MAKEOVER ACADEMY

	Monday	Tuesday	Wednesday	Thursday	Friday	Saturday	Sunday
PREP	Furniture hire delivery __/__	__/__	Pressure washing __/__	Lawns mowed __/__	House clean & windows clean inside & out __/__	Fresh mulch delivery __/__	__/__
PREP	__/__	Photography __/__	__/__	__/__	Marketing live on internet Install signboard __/__	First OFI Utilise Tips and Task Checklist __/__	__/__
WEEK 1	__/__	__/__	OFI Tips & Tasks ☐ OFI time____ __/__	Lawns mowed __/__	Cleaner __/__	OFI Tips & Tasks ☐ OFI time____ __/__	__/__
WEEK 2	__/__	__/__	OFI Tips & Tasks ☐ OFI time____ __/__	Lawns mowed __/__	Cleaner __/__	OFI Tips & Tasks ☐ OFI time____ __/__	__/__
WEEK 3	__/__	__/__	OFI Tips & Tasks ☐ OFI time____ __/__	Lawns mowed __/__	Cleaner __/__	OFI Tips & Tasks ☐ OFI time____ __/__	__/__
WEEK 4	__/__	__/__	OFI Tips & Tasks ☐ OFI time____ __/__	Lawns mowed __/__	Cleaner __/__	Auction Day __/__	__/__

Rightsize Your Home – The Empty Nester's Guide To A Stress-Free Downsize

Feathering The Nest – New Nesters' Success Stories

I want to introduce you to some friends and some of the clients we have helped, and tell you about how they are feeling after their Rightsize. These people now have a home which suits their current needs, they are still in touch with their family and enjoying their company, and they are finding that living in their property is a whole lot less stressful!

I hear that life as a Rightsizer can be so much more fun! Whether you are still working or you are enjoying the fully retired life, the home that you need is a Rightsized one.

I posed the following questions to those who had made the move...

1. *What three main challenges or concerns held you back from making the move from your family home?*
2. *What finally made you make 'the decision' to start planning and do it?*
3. *What do you wish you had known before you started the project, and what would you have done differently?*
4. *Do you believe you left it longer than you should have?*
5. *What are you doing now as a Rightsizer?*
6. *What are the 3 best things about your Rightsized life and why?*
7. *What should you not have worried about?*

Here are some case studies where these questions are answered by Rightsizers themselves. We will begin with Nigel and Ursula.

Nigel and Ursula have worked their entire life in Sydney. Nigel ran his own business and Ursula worked for a long time as an employee of another company. Now they are living their dream, enjoying life as travellers, discovering all different parts of the world. Here is what Nigel had to say:

"We moved from the family home some years ago with the girls going their own way, and left behind the maintenance of the property and gardens etc. I have never had a problem disposing of items no longer needed by selling, giving them away or dumping, so gradually trimmed things down to some easily stored items. This has enabled us to become footloose to do what we like best, which is travelling.

So in the past 18 months I estimate we have travelled 160,000kms, by trains, boats, planes, and the motorhome, visiting some 24 countries. So that is what I call Rightsize for now - we can go where we want, when we want, and later, when we are even older, we will buy somewhere quiet requiring minimum maintenance.

The problem then will be not enough "stuff" but we can steal it from the girls (don't tell them)."

***

Gwen recently sold her larger property, has completed a private purchase of a smaller property that she had renovated, and is now enjoying her own space and again travelling, often with friends.

"One of the worrying things was the housing market being depressed, especially for the sale of my price range of property. Also the enormity of the whole operation - overwhelming! And the timing of the renovations of my cottage making it habitable for me to move into.

I finally made the decision to make the move before the maintenance of the garden and property became too much for me. I began to wonder why I was doing all this work for ME! I was also fairly isolated, with few visitors. The grandchildren were starting to grow up and have weekend commitments so I was not seeing them as much as I used to. So why continue living in such a large property?

I wish I had known previously I was capable of moving through the process. With a little help and encouragement from Belinda, I knew the timing was right.

I am enjoying renovating and seeing the results while creating a beautiful little cottage and garden. I loved creating MY cottage and garden from scratch and having the design, colour scheme, layout etc. the way I want it."

***

Albert and his wife made a move from a three bedroom unit with stairs to a smaller house on a level block just recently. Here is what Albert had to say:

"My biggest challenge was I had too much stuff! I was not sure how to handle it and found it quite overwhelming. I really needed to do the downsize because I worried if anything happened to my wife or I, I wanted to know I could manage or be able to care for her.

What I wish I had done differently was I should have done it earlier. In fact, I should have come to the place I am in now 12 years earlier and not had another move in between. Life as a Rightsizer is really good. We have got rid of a whole lot more stuff and we are on a level block, it's all easier to manage.

We shouldn't have worried that the whole project wouldn't come together. It did and it worked really well."

Marion moved from a five bedroom home to a three bedroom apartment. She had an enormous Rightsize project, but got through it and is now thoroughly enjoying the next stage of her life.

"We loved our home so much, the beach lifestyle, garden and friends made it hard to leave. Also finding a place that would accept my dog was a major challenge.

The final 'push' was our financial situation. We knew we should have made a decision earlier. I actually wish we had sold the year before, mainly because my husbands' health was failing. We definitely left it too long to move, yes, without a doubt.

I love going out every day and travelling, I just got back from India! I love spending more time with friends, going out to lunch, as well as enjoying Bridge and visiting my nearest clubs often.

We achieved the price we needed to and comfortably bought our new home. We managed to transition smoothly with little stress. I would not have been able to do it without Belinda's crew and the help she provided on every level!

Styling The New Property

You are in the driver's seat of your new stylish pad! We love having the opportunity to help our new Rightsizers entirely re-think their style and requirements for their new property.

With the 'change' that comes from making the next move (and the new life chapter), we always help our Rightsizers realise their unique style and help them purchase modern furnishings and create an entirely new look.

When you do the numbers, the interior furnishings have the same 'value questions' applied. We are often asked to replace many items.

Imagine how much it would cost to lift, transport and unpack these items that you are thinking of replacing and might not like anymore.

Our top items of replacement also double as the pre-sale or pre-rental presentation exercise. If you are very organised and are not going on the property market in a rush, then the beauty of this situation is that you have time to get the right advice and purchase some new contemporary items. Purchasing items that you love for your next place will also mean that you do not have to pay the full furniture hire costs to come presentation time. It's exciting for our clients to be able to do a lovely update, spend some money and end up saving some cash. With guidance, you can get whatever you want.

The items that we usually purchase are:
- Lounge and cushions
- Beds
- Linen and cushions
- Artwork
- Outdoor furniture
- Plants and pots

Our standard requirements for a makeover at the new property are a complement to the entire purchase plan of furnishings used at the previous home, i.e., all of the decisions are completed as a holistic project. These lovely items can be taken to your new home, as per the allocation on the floor plan. They will all work well with existing pieces to create a lovely effect.

If the next property is not brand new, we are also involved in changes there, such as:

- Painting
- Window furnishings
- Lighting
- And anything else that takes your fancy!

Styling is the fun side of the project where we get to the finish line and at the same time a new beginning. Time and time again, I have seen the enormous sigh of relief from our clients as they enjoy a drink on their new deck. *"Why didn't we do this sooner?"* is the usual line. *"I just can't believe that we did this." "You people are amazing; we could never have done this without you."* Ok, ok, I know. That last one I slipped in there as a bit of flagrant self-promotion, but it just makes me so very happy and proud to see that we, in some way, have played a part in changing people's lives for the better.

The Final Case For Rightsizing

I was compelled to write this book because I see far too many people missing out on the joys of leading a Rightsized life.

Time and again, I see middle-aged Australians who have become sick and tired of maintaining the family home. They may even be living frugally and coping with a massive amount of stress, *and for what reason?*

Over the years, I have come across the same problems with an all -fit-to-one solution, and that is transitioning and finding a more appropriate-sized home. I love my job because I am not only helping to transform homes, but I am also helping to transform lives in the process, and this is the thing I enjoy the most.

I love seeing the Empty Nesters' properties being sold, or leased, to a younger family, and I love helping them settle in and makeover their new stylish abode!

I love hearing their conversations about what they are going to do every day and where they are going to go with the new-found freedom of their downsized lifestyle. I enjoy their fun comments about not looking after the maintenance problems and spending their time and money elsewhere, discussing the things they love doing the most.

I have seen so many success stories of smaller home private purchases, grey nomads, retirement living, over 55's and I am looking forward to helping more clients who choose to Rightsize their life.

By reading this book, I hope you have come to the same conclusion that I have: Rightsizing your home should be your foremost priority if you do wish to maintain your well-being and make the most out of your retirement.

There is no need to carry the stress of owning a family home you can no longer manage. If you are paying for others to maintain your property, you are giving away your hard-earned money, and it will not be helping you get anywhere fast.

If I can motivate just one Empty Nester to step into the Rightsizing zone and enter into an exciting new Rightsizing chapter earlier in their lives by reading this book, then I will feel like I have done my job!

Where To From Here?

Thank you very much for taking the time to read my book. It was a pleasure writing it, and I'm thrilled to have shared my thoughts and insights with you. I trust you found it highly valuable and feel inspired about the exciting and rewarding times ahead.

Stop holding back! It's time to get out and about and investigate the options, determine your wants and needs, find out the facts and openly communicate with your inner circle. It's a team effort, but remember you are still in control.

I hope I have inspired you to feel motivated and ready enough to plan, organise, move and style your next property move at this vital time in your life. I want all young-at-heart Rightsizers to feel guilt-free and excited about enjoying this stage and the fun things that await you.

So come on. *What are you waiting for?*

Get Rightsized now for a better life.

Belinda x

About Belinda Woolrych

Belinda Woolrych is a keynote speaker and commentator on Pre-Sale Property Styling and Downsizing. Belinda is a woman with a deep passion for helping guide and motivating people to make the right decisions when going about their property transition.

Belinda has built her successful and reputable brand - belindawoolrych.com and Property Makeover Academy - over the last decade and has gained an incredible insight into downsizing along the way, much of which she has shared in this book. Belinda has also contributed to the community by sharing her knowledge and in many other ways.

These businesses have been built on the foundation of Belinda's boundless enthusiasm and drive to help homeowners make one of the most significant moves of their lives: to get their property on the market for sale or lease more profitably and into their Rightsized home, so they can make the most out of their retirement.

A key to Belinda's success is her ability to identify precisely what the target market is looking for and to helping her clients realise the maximum property sale or rental potential.

Before entering the property industry, Belinda forged a successful 16-year career with one of Australia's largest retailers, spending most of that time in training and change management. She holds a Postgraduate Diploma in Management Cert IV, and a Diploma in Training & Assessment, and a Professional Diploma in Interior Design. This blend of practical experience and formal qualifications has provided Belinda with a solid platform from which to deliver a personalised, well-informed and highly reputable service to this niche property market.

Belinda is available to speak at conferences and regularly speaks at Rightsizing Seminars, and is in many homes with her Rightsizing training packages.

If you liked the book, and also help service Downsizers, *why not order in bulk?*

To find out more about Belinda Woolrych and the services she offers, please visit:

www.rightsizeyourhome.com.au
www.propertymakeoveracademy.com.au

Facebook www.facebook.com/rightsizeyourhome
LinkedIn www.linkedin.com/showcase/rightsize-your-home

"I didn't hold back from taking their services because Belinda was recommended by Geoff Grist, our fantastic agent from R&W in Mosman. Belinda had a degree of organisation of which I would have been incapable myself. I would recommend them to anyone inexperienced in the travails and tragedies of house flogging!"

Julian Short, Mosman

"We recently hired Belinda and her team to come into our 90-year-old neighbour's home and get it ready for sale. It was in original state and Belinda and her amazing team were able to transform it in just days. We are forever grateful for meeting Belinda Woolrych and forever grateful for all the help she gave us."

Simone

"Belinda offered some great suggestions on what we could do to improve our property prior to sale. She understood we didn't have a lot of time nor money to invest in preparing for sale and was able to point out those improvements which would have maximum impact. Her critique of our home was thoughtful and constructive."

Sheryn, Cromer

"I was very anxious about 'the move" and hoped I would be able to find people who were in touch with my needs as an individual, and who would treat my property with care. Belinda and her team were calm, sensitive and totally understanding."

Margaret

"Sold in two weeks for the price we were after... what more can you say than that? If you are looking to sell your home fast, then working with Belinda is the solution. You will have an attractive home that people will fall in love with and just 'have' to buy."

Joanna

"Belinda Woolrych is an easy person to deal with. She is passionate about her business & providing a quality service to her clients. She understands the boundaries of giving feedback about improving a home without being critical of individual tastes."

Jo, Pymble

"I used Belinda to style my unit. It went up for sale on the weekend and sold for an amount far exceeding expectations. Every person commented on how fabulous it looked. Highly recommend her services for those thinking about selling."

Sal Knight

"Belinda Woolrych and her team have been exceptional in their management and property preparation. A particular vendor was reluctant to move after 40 years in their much-loved family home. From an original run down brick home, Belinda inexpensively transformed this property into a clean, fresh and more desirable home, done precisely to appeal to a specific demographic of buyer."

Andrew Strong, LJ Hooker

"You gave us wonderful ideas on how to present the house for sale. It was no longer our home but a 'business transaction' and we took your ideas on board and worked very hard to create a beautiful house for sale."

Janice

"As a stay-at-home dad with two boys and a wife in a professional I.T Job, I can say I needed a few tips on the house keeping. Out of all the things Belinda Woolrych did for us, the best thing was their suggestion for me to put up a new washing line and where."

Bill, Newport

"We sold our home to the first buyer that inspected it, even before it was officially listed on the market! We would recommend Belinda Woolrych to anyone looking to sell their home, or simply improve the interior design of their current home."

Rebecca

BONUS RESOURCE
Your Moving Checklist

☑	Action	Responsibility	Date Completed	Notes
	1-2 Months Before Move			
	Pick your moving date. NOTE: Mondays - Thursdays are best choices so that banks and offices are open in case you have a problem			
	Create binder/folder for moving records (estimates, receipts, inventory lists, etc)			
	Plan your moving method (truck rental, hiring movers, etc) and get cost estimates			
	Conduct an inventory of your belongings			
	Research storage facilities if needed			
	Schedule disconnection/ connection of utilities at old and new place:			
	* We recommend ConnectNow to help you			
	NOTE: They usually require up to 5 business days notice in advance			
	[ ] Phone			
	[ ] Internet			

Copyright © 2020. Rightsize Your Home. All rights reserved.

☑	Action	Responsibility	Date Completed	Notes
	1-2 Months Before Move			
	[ ] Cable			
	[ ] Water			
	[ ] Gas			
	[ ] Electrical			
	Plan how you will move vehicles, plants, pets and valuables. ConnectNow can organise this			
	Plan how you will arrange furniture in the new place - use a floor plan or sketch. We can help you!			

Copyright © 2020. Rightsize Your Home. All rights reserved.

☑	Action	Responsibility	Date Completed	Notes
	1-2 Months Before Move			
	Hold a garage sale, donate, sell, recycle, rubbish unnecessary items			
	Schedule transfer of records (medical, children in school, etc)			
	Get copies of any records needed (medical, dental, etc)			
	Acquire packing materials:			
	* We recommend HireABox. Enter our promotional code PSR10			
	[ ] moving boxes			
	[ ] waterproof markers, felt tip markers, coloured markers			
	[ ] plastic bags (different sizes and colours)			
	[ ] bubblewraps, newsprint, other cushioning material			
	[ ] scissors or utility knife			
	[ ] packing tape			
	[ ] trolley			

Copyright © 2020. Rightsize Your Home. All rights reserved.

☑	Action	Responsibility	Date Completed	Notes
	1-2 Months Before Move			
	[ ] ropes			
	Make any home repairs that you have committed to making			
	Return borrowed, check-out or rented items			
	Get things back that you have lent out			
	Start using up food you have stored so there is less to move			

Copyright © 2020. Rightsize Your Home. All rights reserved.

3-4 Weeks Before Move

☑ Action	Responsibility	Date Completed	Notes
Finalise moving method and make necessary arrangements			
Begin packing non-essential items			
Label boxes by room and contents for your next home's designated area			
Separate keys and valuable items to transport yourself - label as DO NOT MOVE			
Keep a box out for storing pieces, parts and essential tools that you will want to keep with you on move day - label as PARTS / DO NOT MOVE			
Create an inventory list of items and box contents, including serial numbers of major items - use this as an opportunity to update your home inventory			
Fill out a Change of Address form at a post office or online. Australia Post offers a Mail Redirection service			

Copyright © 2020. Rightsize Your Home. All rights reserved.

	3-4 Weeks Before Move			
☑	Action	Responsibility	Date Completed	Notes
	Provide important contacts with your new address:			
	[ ] Employers			
	[ ] Family & Friends			
	[ ] Accountant			
	[ ] Australian Electoral Commission			
	[ ] Centrelink			
	[ ] State Road and Maritime Services			
	[ ] Landlord/Real Estate Agent			
	[ ] Solicitors/Lawyer			
	[ ] Councils/Pet Registration			
	[ ] Others			

Copyright © 2020. Rightsize Your Home. All rights reserved.

☑	Action	Responsibility	Date Completed	Notes
	Notify your insurance and credit card companies about change of address			
	Cancel automated payment plans and local accounts / memberships if necessary			
	Take your vehicle(s) in for a tune-up, particularly if you are relocating far			

3-4 Weeks Before Move

Copyright © 2020. Rightsize Your Home. All rights reserved.

☑	Action	Responsibility	Date Completed	Notes
	1-2 Weeks Before Move			
	Continue packing and clean as you go			
	Pack items separately that you will need right away at your new place			
	Plan to take the day off for moving day			
	Find useful things for your children to do - involve them as much as possible			
	Find someone to help watch small children on move day			
	Begin to pack your suitcases with clothes and personal items for the trip			
	Reconfirm your method of moving with those involved			
	Make sure your prescriptions are filled			
	Empty out your safe deposit box, secure those items for safe travel			

Copyright © 2020. Rightsize Your Home. All rights reserved.

☑	Action	Responsibility	Date Completed	Notes
	Schedule cancellation of services for your old place:			
	[ ] Newspaper			
	[ ] House cleaning			
	[ ] Lawn			
	[ ] Pool			
	[ ] Water Delivery			
	Check your furniture for damages - note damages on your inventory			
	Take furniture apart if necessary (desks, shelves, etc.) or ensure this job is on your removalist list			
	Make sure all paperwork for the old and new place is complete			
	If traveling far, notify credit card company to prevent automated deactivation			
	Appropriately dispose of flammables such as paint, propane, and gasoline			
	Use up food, with focus on perishable foods			

Copyright © 2020. Rightsize Your Home. All rights reserved.

☑	Action	Responsibility	Date Completed	Notes
	2-4 Days Before Move			
	Confirm all moving details and that you have necessary paperwork			
	Make a schedule or action plan for the day of the move			
	Plan when/how to pick up the truck (if rented)			
	Prepare for the moving expenses (moving, food, lodging)			
	Continue cleaning the house as you are packing			
	Defrost your freezer and clean the fridge			
	Make sure essential tools are handy (screwdrivers, pliers, tape, etc)			
	Pack a bag for water bottles, pen/paper, snacks, documents, and essentials			
	Set aside boxes/items that you are moving yourself (make sure you'll have room)			

Copyright © 2020. Rightsize Your Home. All rights reserved.

☑	Action	Responsibility	Date Completed	Notes
	Moving Day			
	Go early to pick up the truck if you rented one			
	Take movers/helpers through the house to inform them of what to do			
	Walk through the empty place to check for things left behind - look behind doors			
	Leave your contact info for new residents to forward mail			
	Take inventory before movers leave, sign bill of lading			
	Make sure your movers have the correct new address			
	Leave the garage door remote, air conditioning remote where it can be easily found (i.e. kitchen counter)			
	Lock the windows and doors, turn off the lights			
	Use a padlock to lock up a rented truck			

Copyright © 2020. Rightsize Your Home. All rights reserved.

At your new place ...

☑	Action	Responsibility	Date Completed	Notes
	Verify utilities are working, eg: power, water, heating, and cooling			
	Perform an initial inspection, note all damages, take photographs if needed			
	Update all insurance details straight away			
	Clean the kitchen and vacuum as needed (especially where furniture will be going)			
	Direct movers/helpers where to put things			
	Pack you and your team drinks and snacks, to stay nourished			
	Assemble beds with bedding			
	Begin unpacking, starting with kitchen, bathroom, bedrooms and other essentials			

Copyright © 2020. Rightsize Your Home. All rights reserved.

☑	Action	Responsibility	Date Completed	Notes
	Moving In - Weeks 1-2			
	Check for damages while unpacking - be aware of deadline for insurance claims			
	Replace locks if necessary and make at least 2 copies of your new keys			
	Confirm that mail is now arriving at your new address			
	Make sure your previous utilities have been paid for and cancelled			
	Complete your change of address checklist			
	[ ] Bank(s)			
	[ ] Credit Cards			
	[ ] Loans			
	[ ] Insurance			
	[ ] Pension Plans			
	[ ] Lawyer/Solicitor			
	[ ] Accountant			

Copyright © 2020. Rightsize Your Home. All rights reserved.

☑	Action	Responsibility	Date Completed	Notes
	Moving In - Weeks 1-2			
	[ ] Family Support			
	[ ] Newspapers			
	[ ] Magazines			
	[ ] Licenses			
	[ ] Memberships			
	Schedule a time to get a local driving license and update vehicle registration			
	Obtain local phonebooks and maps			
	Find new doctors, dentists, etc, depending on your needs			
	After you have moved in, update your home inventory, including photos of rooms			

Copyright © 2020. Rightsize Your Home. All rights reserved.

Notes

Notes

www.ingramcontent.com/pod-product-compliance
Lightning Source LLC
Chambersburg PA
CBHW070551010526
44118CB00012B/1288